Playing
with
Matches

Also by Michael Faudet

Dirty Pretty Things
Bitter Sweet Love
Smoke & Mirrors
Winter of Summers
Cult of Two

Playing
with
Matches

Michael Faudet

Andrews McMeel
PUBLISHING®

For my Readers,

*Who have traveled on this magical journey with me
and continue to inspire my writing today.*

INTRODUCTION

Playing with Matches is my sixth book and a desperate escape from the tyranny of now.

A moment in time to reflect on the extraordinary journey my previous books have taken me on.

A rare opportunity to revisit the past and curate the poetry and prose that still spark my imagination.

Sprinkled with new pieces of writing that capture my conflicting emotions—a pendulum swinging between happiness and despair in the age of the pandemic.

However, the real inspiration for the book came from a rather different place.

My love of roses.

Delicate explosions of red bursting out of a black glass vase.

A hint of perfume that softly speaks of illicit sex.

Every petal unfurled—a poet.

Every thorn—a pen.

Extraordinary flowers that write a beautiful final verse.

Transforming even the act of dying into an exquisite art.

—

Playing with Matches is my gift to the dreamers and the fatalists.

But most of all, it's a book for my wonderful readers.

Love always,

Michael xo

THE BEGINNING OF THE END

*She had a mind like a box of fireworks and hands
that played recklessly with matches.*

DOLPHINS

You are my every morning—
   a waking dream reflected
   in sleepy eyes.

Black coffee poured
   with shortbread biscuits.

The cat meowing
   to be fed.

Back to bed—
   you say.

My hands resting
   on your hips,
   staring at the view
   outside our window.

Dolphins swimming
   in the bay.

WONDERFULLY RIGHT

I certainly know right from wrong, she said, but the trouble is, whenever I feel your hands unclipping my bra—wrong suddenly feels wonderfully right.

Swept Away

You were the sea
    that swept me away,
    only to leave
    me adrift—
    far from the shore,
    my legs
    growing tired
    of the lies
    that you said,
    out of my depth—
    in deep water
    I tread.

THE NORTHERN LIGHTS

She was like the northern lights on a cloudless night. Walking toward me, leaving a trail of dark footsteps on the silvery sand. The waves breaking gently behind her, white foamy fingers reaching out and caressing her ankles with swirling salty kisses. Beads of glistening water clinging to her naked body, dusty pink nipples hard, skin ghostly pale, a single strand of wet black hair curled like a comma across her blushing cheeks.

—

"I want you to fuck me," she whispered. "It is far too beautiful an evening to make love."

Believe

"I believe in you." Words that water flowers.

I Am Tired

I am tired
    of feeling tired.

Tired of crying,
    while I write
    this verse.

Tired of this endless
    creepy crawly
    inner torment.

Tossing and turning,
    unable to sleep.

Tired of thinking,
    always thinking.

That maybe,
    just maybe—

You've become
    tired of me too.

LISTEN TO YOUR HEART

Nobody knows your heart better than you. Trust your instincts. Never let anyone cast a shadow over your sunshine.

I Am the Girl

In the quiet times—
    when I think about my life,
    you come to me,
    banging pots and pans
    inside my head,
    your voice screaming—
    I am the girl
    you'll never forget.

Teach Me

Such pretty things
    you said to me—
    unbutton me
    some more.

For I am yours
    to take tonight
    upon this forest floor.

Let's make a bed
    in autumn leaves,
    and leave
    no leaf unturned.

Beneath these trees
    please teach me,
    please—

To learn a love
    unlearned.

Arabian Dawn

She possessed a rare beauty that was slowly revealed with every word she spoke—like how an Arabian dawn softly breaks the darkness with the gentlest of hands.

IF ONLY

If only wishes were as reliable as disappointment.

TURNED ON

Oh, when it comes to being turned on, she said, it's simple. You have to first unbutton my mind before unclipping my bra.

WE SPOKE

We spoke of love
  and cities found,
  of buried gold
  deep underground,
  how rivers sigh
  when lost to sea,
  of whiskey poured
  in cups of tea.

We spoke of art
  in golden frames,
  of memories lost,
  forgotten names,
  how shooting stars
  write wishes bright,
  and shadows fade
  into the night.

We spoke of wolves
  and many things,
  of ticking clocks
  and circus swings,
  how crying doves
  fly up above,
  but most of all
  we spoke of love.

TWISTED TREES

A fearsome wind
    cannot compel
    the weakest branch
    to gladly yield.

Yet,
    the faintest breath
    upon your lips—
    and I have fallen
    against my will.

SELF-RIGHTEOUS

I have always found self-righteous people to be obsessed with *self* and seldom *righteous*.

She Said

"Romance is all well and good, but . . . it's just that I am not in the mood for whispered sweet nothings or your fingers running softly through my hair. What I want, more than anything, is for you to treat me like your own personal sex doll.

"Don't kiss me—make me bite my lip."

A Lighthouse in a Storm

It was a love that defied the change of seasons, the ebb and flow of tides, the transition from day to night—a lighthouse in a storm.

Trigger Warning

There is no trigger warning,
    when the gunman
    pulls the trigger.

No safe space,
    when a bullet takes a life.

No sanity,
    when insanity is elected.

And no humanity,
    when the rifle
    is protected—
    but not the child.

The Last Days of Summer

Perhaps it was the rhythmic chant of cicadas that lulled me into this calm state of being. The last days of summer—in all its glorious sunsets and fading colors. Nature's delightful, intoxicating narcotic. Freeing my mind from the chaos of simply breathing.

ROSES

Roses wear blindfolds,
  Violets crack whips,
  candle wax dripping,
  teeth biting lips.

THE RIVER BANK

It was a gin and tonic kind of lazy summer's day. Pleasantly warm with just a hint of lavender in the air. One of those languid, do-nothing kind of afternoons, sitting under the old willow tree, its weeping branches reaching out and caressing the cool waters of the muddy riverbank.

Morphine's slender fingers danced a gentle waltz through her sister's ash-blond hair, turning the wispy strands of silvery yellow into perfect braids that fell across bare shoulders of milky white.

Opium quietly took a sip from her tall glass, stopping only to wince when Morphine pulled a little too hard on an errant lock that had tried to escape her busy hands.

Heroin, the eldest of the three, blew smoke rings into the air, flicking the ash from the freshly rolled joint onto the soft blanket of grass. She instantly knew from the very first toke that this particular harvest from her father's latest crop was destined to be, using his words, "a vintage year."

"My turn, my turn, pass it over here, H," said Opium in her singsong voice, her arm outstretched and finger comically beckoning for the joint.

Heroin took another deep lungful of smoke before handing it over and reaching for the manuscript that sat beside her. A collection of neatly typed pages, all ring-bound and written by her esteemed father, who lectured in biology and botany at Spectre Hall University.

When he wasn't teaching and writing books, Professor Estrange spent his idle days focused on his real passion in life: growing rare orchids and cultivating mind-enhancing new strains of marijuana.

"Yummy, yummy, yummy," cried Opium, a crooked smile slowly creeping across her pretty face. She watched as a spiraling column of bluish smoke rose up from her rosy lips and faded into the gentle breeze.

None of the girls heard the footsteps, and they were pleasantly startled when Serena appeared from behind them.

"Well then, what do we have here? A pretty young wolf on the hunt for helpless lambs," said Heroin, laughing.

Serena drifted silently to the ground, her summer dress forming a pool of swirling white cotton upon the sea of green. Her slender arm wrapping itself around Heroin's naked shoulders, lips kissing lips.

"You two should get a room," sniggered Opium, blowing a large plume of smoke into the air.

"You're just jealous," Morphine replied, poking her sister hard in the ribs with a perfectly manicured finger. "Now sit still. I've got one more braid to do."

"Ouch! You can be such a fucking bitch, M."

Opium angrily pulled herself away from Morphine's busy hands and stood up. She took a deep toke on the dying joint and flicked it away, sending it spiraling into the river.

Heroin ran a finger gently down Serena's cheek, tracing a line across her wet lips, the two lovers completely oblivious to Opium's little hissy fit.

Morphine gathered up the empty glasses and started to pack them away in a wicker basket, along with the half-empty bottle of gin. The unwelcome visit by a determined wasp, hovering, landing, and hovering again, made Opium giggle.

"I hope it stings you," she said, laughing as Morphine tried to shoo the unwanted visitor away. Serena glanced up at Opium and flashed her a smile. "How's tricks, O?"

"Well, I was all fine and dandy before my witch of a sister decided to break my ribs," Opium replied.

Morphine laughed and picked up the basket. "Time to leave these two alone. Come on, you cry baby."

Opium reluctantly took Morphine's outstretched hand, and the two sisters departed silently, like two ghosts lost in a forest of swaying trees and humming dragonflies.

—

Serena watched the sun melt into the distance, the river taking on an eerie orange hue, painting the reeds with long, dark shadows. She was naked. The white dress folded neatly by her side, a pair of crumpled pink panties hanging on a branch.

"It's so beautiful here," she sighed.

Heroin was already dressed, a joint freshly lit, sitting cross-legged, one hand flicking through her father's manuscript. She looked up, took another toke, and blew a perfect smoke ring.

"Then why are you leaving? What's so important about New York, anyway?"

A flotilla of ducks glided across the water. Serena stared blankly at them. She could feel the tears starting to run down her cheeks.

"I love you, H, and perhaps I always will."

——

The Diary of Heroin Estrange. June 8, 1998

If my ink were tears, would this pen never stop writing?

I cannot begin to fathom the intricate nature of love, the endless "whys" and the cold reality of "because." My restless heart held ransom by circumstance, left to drown in a river on a perfect summer's day. The memory of your kisses still fresh upon my lips.

Can a blade not cut any deeper into my pale wrists?

Your parting words, my life flowing from me. The pain unbearable. Overwhelming.

Only the echo of your laughter left behind to taunt me, a constant reminder of the happiness we once shared. Your body entwined in mine, all warmth fading as the minutes turn to hours.

Oh, to be numb. To escape the cruel torment of such bittersweet love.

There is no perfect ending to a relationship.

No magic formula.

Just a silent scream as they rip your fucking heart out.

Desperation

We held on to our dream so tightly that not even reality could take it away.

Away from You

I think of thoughts
    that cannot be,
    no hand can reach
    across this sea,
    the seasons change
    on distant shores,
    from frosty skies
    to sunshine blue,
    as summer's touch
    undresses you—

Reminding me
    of all the things
    I often wish,
    but cannot do.

Isolation

If only we could escape the prying eyes and virtuous finger-wagging of this small-town circus.

To run away and hide our love in some distant foreign city. Where the past ceases to exist and freedom is found in the company of strangers.

Until then, let's just close the shutters, bolt the door, and switch off the lights.

And kiss in the dark shadows of glorious isolation.

Uncharted

Think of me as an uncharted map. I want your hands to explore every single city, town, and village.

.

Lost

Lost is a lovely place to find yourself.

A Midnight Call

Be careful—
someone might be listening.

I can almost hear
that rebellious smile
in your silent reply.

The one you wear
so well on rosy lips.

Your hushed moans
begin again,
becoming louder.

Pretty mouth—
pressed up against
the hotel phone.

Encore

I love to watch you touch yourself,
    on rainy afternoons.

The wandering hands.

The soft little moans.

Hips twitching,
    wet fingers fucking.

A solo show
    performed for one.

I Hear You

I know there are times when you think I'm not listening. Lost in my own little world of self-denial. But believe me, I do hear your words—and your undying love for me is like a hand pressed into my back. Pushing me forward. All the encouragement I will ever need.

Curious Girl

She was a curious girl,
    who loved the smell
    of old books,
    chasing butterflies,
    and touching herself
    under the covers.

Lost Words

A midnight scribble,
    a morning sigh,
    you watch the words
    curl up and die.

Madness lives
    inside your head,
    of poems lost
    and pages dead.

A mind possessed,
    by unmade books,
    unwritten lines
    on empty hooks.

ONLY YOU COULD WRITE

A wave explodes—
    the slow rumble
    of thunder,
    swirling sand,
    and seaweed.

A paperback novel—
    resting on a bed
    of broken seashells,
    the pages open—
    a sentence underlined
    in pencil gray.

You kiss me—
    the scent of weed
    lingering on lips,
    only you could
    write a sunset
    this beautiful.

Holding hands
    beneath tangerine skies,
    a sea of rolling fire
    and flying fish,
    a daydream made real—
    in the shutter click
    of an eyelid.

ECHO

I am hopelessly in love with a memory. An echo from another time, another place.

A Tired Butterfly

Our love—
    a tired butterfly
    trapped in a glass jar,
    wings beating
    like two hearts
    refusing to let go,
    oblivious—
    to the reality
    of fate,
    disguised
    as hope.

Firecracker

The stuttering chime
    of a broken alarm clock
    waking me at midnight.

A barking dog—
    chasing ghosts
    in my garden.

The Beach Boys singing
    "God Only Knows"
    on repeat.

A forgotten white sock
    spinning in the dryer.

The beautiful decay
    of reason and logic,
    held together—
    by the pour
    of a bottomless
    vodka bottle.

I once called you
    my little firecracker.

Lighting the fuse—
    but not knowing
    when to let go.

LOVE DEFINED

Burn all the dictionaries, tear up the tired metaphors, and tell the poets to go to hell. For you are the true definition of love. The only one I shall ever need.

The Silence

On a good day
    I could hear a pin drop,
    the distant humming
    of a bumblebee,
    a soapy bubble
    popping in a bath.

But somehow,
    I didn't hear
    the deafening roar
    of my heart breaking.

Just the silence
    when you were gone.

By the Sea

I dreamt of us last night, living in the little stone cottage by the sea, the one you promised me.

Our love held together by wrinkled hands as we slowly walked across ever-sinking sands. Each languid step taking us closer toward our very last sunset.

It wasn't until I was fully awake that I truly woke up.

I suddenly realized it's no coincidence the two middle letters of life are *if*.

For every action we make, there is a reaction. The outcome often beyond our control, fragile and fraught with ruinous consequences. Like a soap bubble made real by a gentle breath only to be taken by it.

If you had stayed here, in my trembling arms, would our fingers not be pricked by the thorns of red roses?

And what if our love could have stood up to the storm, standing strong, like our cottage by the sea?

If only . . .

We Wrote

We wrote about love—our sentences the hands that caressed each other on warm summer nights. A story without an ending, written by a pen that would never run dry.

Passing Seconds

How I love the slow seduction of the now. The moment when even passing seconds take a deep breath and all that matters is your eyes staring into mine.

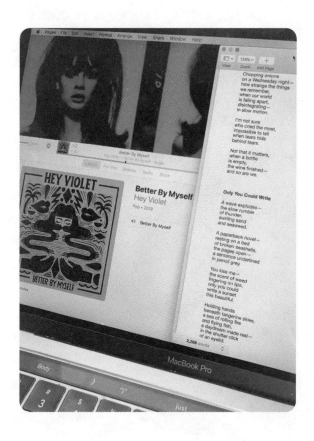

Spellbound

The very suggestion
    of your words, she said—
    bind my wrists tighter
    than any rope.

SHARJAH

My love for you—
    comes from a place
    where stars sing
    to strangers,
    and desert sands
    hold the sea
    in a delicate
    embrace,
    under a crescent moon
    your kisses sweet—
    lips sprinkled
    with sugar dust,
    pale pink,
    rosewater-infused
    rahat lokum.

Where magic
    wakes with the dawn,
    the morning call
    to prayer—
    if scent made a sound
    it would be this,
    the rarest
    of perfumes.

It is here
    from a city of books,
    my love for you
    is written.

Parked on the Street

You had reached that trembling point. My fingers gently rubbing your hard clitoris, slowly pushing you over the edge. Your eyes closing—pussy lips dripping wet. Hard nipples pressed up against a steamy side window. Skirt hitched up. Panties wrapped around one ankle.

My hand feeling you cum in the back seat of a VW Beetle.

THE BOARDWALK

I often found myself wandering along the creaky wooden boardwalk that lined a sandy beach of setting sun and loved-up couples clutching last-minute ice creams. The dripping cones ignored between hurried kisses and selfie shots taken with crooked horizons.

A kaleidoscope of constantly changing images moving in time with each step taken.

A lone Ferris wheel turning slowly in the distance. The squawking of angry seagulls fighting over the last thrown french fry. A wispy trail of grayish smoke curling up from a group of huddled skaters, the sweet aroma of pot and half-eaten hot dogs. A gorgeous girl with auburn hair, reading a well-worn copy of *Brighton Rock*. An elderly man sitting next to her, wearing an olive-green suit and a sleepy white terrier lying by his feet. The muted thunder of crashing waves, sparkles of dappled light dancing across the restless ocean. Sugary doughnuts placed into pretty, pink paper bags by the Polish lady who never smiled, her gaudy purple-and-green-striped stand surrounded by a bunch of screaming children.

Suddenly, something new but strangely familiar caught my eye.

A shop window, filled with dusty headless mannequins, dressed formally in chic vintage clothing and antique jewelry. The sign above the door said "Under New Management," written in red cursive lettering. A hypnotic trickle of Billie Holiday singing

"Blue Moon," flowing from two tinny outdoor speakers.

Somehow, I felt drawn to this place, an overwhelming feeling of belonging taking me by the hand and pulling me inside—or maybe it was just the codeine kicking in. I had taken two extra-strength tablets before leaving home. To calm a restless late-afternoon hangover and take advantage of that wonderful, almost detached, floaty euphoric existence that the little white pills conjured up.

A tinkling silver bell rang above my head as I pushed open the squeaky door and entered the shop. My eyes blinking, adjusting to the low light, slowly taking in the cluttered shelves and crowded floor space, filled with all manner of treasures and curiosities.

A statue of the Virgin Mary wrapped in flashing colored fairy lights stood silently in the corner. Wooden shelves lined the walls, filled with wonderful old books, pristine 1960s *Playboy* magazines, various pieces of poster art, unscratched vintage toys, and a taxidermy fox with an amazingly intact bushy tail. In fact, everything seemed in perfect, mint condition for its age.

Inside an ornate cabinet, there was a butterfly collection pinned to a yellow canvas and enclosed behind glass, surrounded by a gold gilt frame.

It was sitting among a collection of novelty mugs, shiny tobacco tins, war medals, and pocketknives with bone handles. I carefully opened the doors to take a closer look. "Can I help you?"

A young woman appeared from behind a heavy red velvet curtain. She was dressed in a black-and-white vintage tuxedo, complete with silk top hat and shiny black patent leather lace-up boots. Her face was a shade of moonlight white, with dark circles around her pretty blue eyes and smiling lips painted purple. It was difficult to guess exactly how old she might be. Somewhere between midtwenties and early thirties maybe. In her hand she held a lit cigarette.

"Oh, I was just checking out the butterflies, the ones in the frame," I replied, a little startled.

She took a long drag from the cigarette, blowing the bluish gray smoke upward.

"African. They're in good condition too. No broken wings. Are you a collector?" she asked.

"No, not really, just curious. My grandfather had something similar—well, I think he did, many years ago."

Her eyes lit up, and she stood to attention, clicking her heels and saluting.

"Hello, my name's Sabrina, and I'm the owner of the shop. Welcome to my alternative world of fascinating yesterdays!"

The words were delivered with an upbeat, almost carnivalesque ring to them, her delicate hand outstretched, waiting for me to shake it, which I did. Her grip firm but gentle, silver rings covering three of her slender fingers.

I felt a tingling in my arm, which was both alarming and pleasant, like a mild electric shock mixed with a relaxing post-massage kind of buzz. Within seconds, this wave of electricity swept through my entire body, making the hairs on the back of my neck rise up.

"Ha! I'm sorry," she laughed, letting go of my hand quickly. "I sometimes have that effect on people." She turned and walked over to the counter and stubbed her cigarette into a circular brass ashtray.

Any thoughts of the framed butterflies quickly vanished, as I clenched my right hand and opened it, repeatedly, trying to rid my fingers of the weird pins and needles feeling.

Sabrina walked over to the front door, turned a key in the lock, and pulled down a black blind. She turned and flashed me a smile. "I think you will be my last customer for the day. Anyway, there are far more thrilling things to do than make small chitchat about African butterflies and stuff."

"Well, I guess I should be on my way," I said awkwardly, not sure what was really happening in this strange little shop.

"No need to rush anywhere," she replied, reaching for my hand. "Come with me, please, I want to show you something pretty amazing."

She took me by the hand and started to lead me toward the back of the shop, past the counter, and toward the red velvet curtain. I didn't resist or feel any more sparks of electricity; I just followed obediently like someone seduced by a dream, never wishing to wake.

The moment I emerged on the other side of the curtain, the last thin shard of reality shattered.

—

My eyes were met with a blinding white light that faded in a split second, reminding me of an old camera flash exploding. As I blinked furiously, the dark circles started to disappear, and the sights and sounds of a café came into full view.

I found myself sitting at a round wooden table covered with a crisp white tablecloth. A cup of black coffee was in front of me, a croissant lay on a white plate by its side, and sitting across from me was Sabrina. The tuxedo outfit had gone, and in its place was a striped tee and a short floral skirt decorated with daisies. A small black leather handbag hung from her chair. She picked up her swirling café au lait and took a sip, her eyes never leaving mine.

A cold panic gripped me, and I felt my chest constrict, my mouth starting to gasp for air.

"Hush now," she laughed, putting her cup down and gently stroking the side of my face. "The adjustment is always a bit freaky the first time. It'll pass. See, you're feeling better already. Now drink your coffee and just relax."

I did as I was told, and she was right. Somehow, the first bite of the strong coffee sent a wave of calmness rippling through me. My heart stopped pounding, and a pleasant sense of peace descended upon me.

I slowly became more aware of my surroundings. Smartly dressed waiters zigzagging between the tables of casually dressed patrons, many engaged in noisy conversations, others hunched over a newspaper. Everyone seemed to be speaking French.

The more I turned my head and looked around, the faster I realized nothing made sense. Not the old cars whizzing along the narrow street or the vintage clothes worn by the pedestrians that strolled past me.

"1964, Saint-Germain, one of my very favorite yesterdays. If you're not going to touch your croissant, I'll have it."

Sabrina didn't wait for a response. She took it quickly from my plate and started to devour it, the buttery, flaky crumbs sticking to her orange lipstick.

So many questions rattled around inside my head, each one seemingly ridiculous and insane. How can you possibly make sense of the impossible?

"I know what you're thinking," she said. "The hows and whys of it all, but believe me, you don't need to know. It just is. I can tell you this much, you will return to your world, but not before we've had a little fun in this one. Come on, let's get out of this joint and take a look around."

I followed her cue and stood up. Sabrina took some crumpled notes from her handbag and slid them under the plate.

The rest of the morning was spent ducking in and out of the various shops that lined the avenue. Bookstores, fashion boutiques, and cute little places that sold all manner of bits and pieces. It was a shopping trip, and it wasn't long before Sabrina was clutching several bags, filled to the brim with what she called "future merchandise."

"I can't resist a bargain," she laughed. "Can you imagine what I can charge for all of this when we return?"

That's when it hit me. The secret to her "alternative world of fascinating yesterdays" shop. Sabrina was a time-traveling entrepreneur who bought in the past and sold in the present. It also explained how the stock in her shop looked so new and in perfect condition.

"It's incredible. How do you do it? How did we travel through time? This is fucking crazy."

Sabrina gave me a quizzical look and then smiled. "No, silly, we didn't time travel anywhere. I just opened the door to a parallel world. There are many doors and countless worlds. I just happen to love this one. It's all about manipulating quantum physics really; when you know how, it's easy but far too complicated to explain in an afternoon. Just think of it as falling down a rabbit hole."

We stopped outside a black door of a narrow terrace house. Sabrina off-loaded the bags into my hands and fumbled around in her handbag. She took out a key and opened the front door, which had a small brass number 42 attached to it.

"Come on inside. It's not much, but I call it home."

I walked inside the short hallway, which opened to a small lounge room. The walls were painted an emerald-green color. Two brown leather chesterfield chairs and a circular coffee table sat on a carpet of lime green. I put the bags down on one of the chairs and followed Sabrina up a set of stairs that led to her bedroom and a bathroom with a rust-stained sink and a claw-foot bath.

She turned on the taps and placed a plug in the bath.

"Now, why not get out of those clothes and freshen up? I'll leave a dressing gown on the bed for you. Place your clothes outside for washing. Oh, and don't drain the bath, I'll use the water after you've finished."

I had long given up questioning anything and watched her walk out of the bathroom.

My naked body sank beneath the hot water. All traces of my hangover had long gone, replaced with a strange euphoria that swept over me. I closed my eyes and focused on a piece of verse, something that I had been struggling to finish.

Love is a rare rose, the perfume intoxicating—
picked by fingers oblivious to the thorns . . .

"I thought you might want this."

Sabrina's voice snapped me out of my thoughts, my eyes opening quickly and hands frantically trying to cover myself.

She was naked.

A bar of purple soap held in one hand and a glass of champagne in the other. I cast my eyes downward, trying not to look at her, the image of her pert breasts replaying over and over in my mind.

"Ha! I never took you for the bashful type, and from the look of it, not every part of you is shy," she laughed.

I could feel myself getting hard, and my hands could barely contain the erection.

Sabrina placed the glass on the floor and stepped into the bath, her long, milky white legs straddling me as she lowered herself into the water. I looked up into her gorgeous blue eyes and let out a deep moan as she took my hard cock with one hand and guided it deep inside her pussy.

The electricity I had felt when I first shook her hand in the shop returned. It was even more intense. She pushed her hips down to meet each thrust of my cock. Her arms wrapped around my neck as we fucked, hard and fast, sending splashes of water flying out of the bath. Sabrina's final scream bouncing off the bathroom walls. Her orgasm triggering a flash of blinding white light.

—

I was woken by the tickling of a small white terrier dog sniffing my face. My sleepy eyes opened, and the old man in the olive-green suit slowly came into view, peering down at me.

"Are you all right, son?" I sat up, my head feeling dizzy, and realized I was lying on the beach, my nakedness covered by a robe with a blue paisley print.

"I think I'm okay," I replied, looking up at the old man.

He gave me a polite nod and continued to walk along the sand, his little dog trotting behind him.

I started to brush the sand from my hair and noticed a large parcel sitting next to me. It was wrapped in brown paper and tied with a black velvet ribbon.

Suddenly my memory came flooding back to me. The shop. Sabrina. The café. A black terrace house. A tiny bathroom. Fucking . . .

And then nothing.

It was like time had been neatly compressed. The hours reduced to minutes. I was back to the reality of a setting sun that hadn't set. The waves breaking behind me, the boardwalk in the distance.

I opened the parcel carefully and discovered the framed African butterfly collection inside with a handwritten note attached to it.

I thought you might like this. A little something from another yesterday. Your grandfather was such a lovely man. Sabrina. xo

P.S. Come by and collect your clothes sometime.

A smile crept across my lips. As the missing piece of verse wrote itself in my mind. The final words written by another's delicate hand.

How can you possibly make sense of the impossible?

Perhaps you don't even try.

—

*Love is a rare rose, the perfume intoxicating—
picked by fingers oblivious to the thorns.*

*A pleasure found
in the sweet pain of discovery,
and when it wilts
how can we refrain?
From bloodying our fingers—
again and again.*

Kindness

Do you know what really turns me on? What I find incredibly sexy? Kindness.

PROXIMITY

We joined the dots
from A to B,
the line we drew
from you to me,
traced empty shores
across the sea,
over mountain top,
past forest tree,
along the roads
and walking tracks,
all bridges burned,
no looking back,
for the love
we have,
no gate can stop,
no barking dog
or bolted lock,
for what is real
is meant to be,
when two hearts
beat—
in proximity.

Exhaustion

I had reached the point of exhaustion. Where even summoning one last breath to blow on the dying embers of our love was beyond me.

The Kiss

Crashing waves on an empty beach,
　　the rhythm of our hearts,
　　two drowning lovers lost at sea,
　　my lips adrift in yours.

WHEN YOU LEFT

I still remember the gentle squeeze of your hand before you said goodbye. Like a little patch of sunshine found on a cold winter's day.

Damaged Goods

Do we not enter this world a little broken? Damaged goods with awkward smiles. Searching for the glue we call love.

Books

My preferred way to travel is not a plane but a book. How wonderful it is to be transported somewhere new without having to leave your bed.

UNDRESS ME

All that you write,
    you know
    it's not right,
    you move me
    with written suggestion.

I know it's absurd,
    to be undressed by a word,
    write me more
    write me more—
    make me yours.

HERDING CATS

You told me to stop letting my emotions run away from me. But how can I? Herding cats in the dark with one arm tied behind my back would be easier than controlling these feelings I have for you.

Deeper

Every time you open your eyes I fall deeper in love with the story they tell.

Last Night

Normally I tend to choose my words carefully when it comes to such delicate matters. However, seeing you now, here in the moonlight, all I can think about is pulling your panties down and fucking you with your socks on.

THE BROOM CLOSET

There was an almost surreal element to Serena's sexual desires. And tonight was no exception. There were no scattered rose petals or tiny lit candles.

Just a trail of strawberry sherbet sprinkled down the hallway. Which I followed until I reached the end point—a broom closet. Where a pink postage note was stuck to the door with the words *Sex lives here* scribbled in green pen.

I took a deep breath and opened the door.

Serena was standing inside. Her naked body lit by a single lightbulb. I could see she had tipped the last remains of the sherbet over her pussy.

She flashed me a mischievous smile and said, "Lick it clean."

Her words were not so much a request but a command. So I did as I was told. I knelt down on the wooden floorboards and roughly parted her pussy lips with my fingers. I began to lick and suck on her clitoris, feeling the tingle of the sherbet on my tongue.

Serena pressed her hips into my face and started to moan. I kept up the rhythm, slow and steady, until I felt her hand tap my shoulder. It was the signal to stop and give her what she so desperately desired.

A good hard fucking.

Now it was my turn to be the boss.

I got up off my knees, stood up, and unbuckled my black leather belt. Threading it through the loops, one by one, until it was free.

Then I gently wrapped the belt around Serena's neck. Slowly tightening the loop so that the buckle pressed down on her throat.

"Are you ready for your present?"

"Yes," she replied, looking directly into my eyes.

I unzipped my fly and gave the belt a firm pull.

Serena gasped.

"I fucking love it!" she cried, her cheeks flushing red.

I forced my hard cock deep inside her tight pussy. Serena bit down on her lip and began to moan loudly.

This just made me want to fuck her even harder. So I lifted Serena up into my arms and felt her legs grip my waist. Pressing her back hard against the wall, I started to slam my cock in and out of her wet pussy.

Sending us both into a sex-crazed frenzy.

Her tits slapping against my chest with every thrust of my cock.

The pleasure intense and uncontrollable.

I watched her pretty mouth slowly open.

The orgasm exploding between her legs.

—

We stood in the hallway.

Catching our breath.

Cum dripping down the inside of Serena's thigh.

I removed the belt from her neck. Tracing the pink line left behind on her pale skin with my finger.

She placed her hands on my shoulders and stared into my eyes. "Do you know what you do to me? How you make me feel?"

"Glad that you married me?" I replied smiling.

Serena laughed. Pulling me closer and pressing her warm lips to my ear.

"Happy anniversary," she whispered.

LOVE ON MUTE

We watched the rain fall
   outside my window,
   wintery gray static
   playing silently
   on a glass television,
   your head resting
   on my shoulder,
   passing a joint
   between lips
   that said nothing
   and everything
   in the same breath.

My Heart

My heart has become a broken compass. Every time I try to leave you, I always find myself running back into your arms.

LOVE

Falling in love is not rational. It's madness. A beautiful, wonderful moment of magnificent insanity.

Perfume

Her perfume reminded me of freshly picked flowers and sticky candy floss, mixed with a gentle hint of debauchery.

A Morning in Paris

She wore the perfume
      of pages turned,
      the scent of old books
      upon delicate fingers,
      a hint of sunshine
      captured within curls
      of windswept hair.

A morning made
      with poetry
      and swirling milk,
      in coffee sipped
      while Paris wakes,
      the words she read
      in dawn's pale light—
      how butter melts
      on warm croissants.

Our Pretend Summer

You always loved to play make-believe on rainy afternoons.

Blue cellophane taped to a bedroom window. Sipping strawberry daiquiris in chipped coffee cups. Basking in the warm glow of a plastic fan heater.

Dreaming of Saint-Tropez beaches and listening to Lana Del Rey. Two misfits in mismatched pajamas. Peeling oranges and fucking with the lights on.

LOCKDOWN

We have become shipwrecked on our own little islands, surrounded by a dangerous sea filled with invisible sharks. Restless castaways—constantly waiting for the next message in a bottle to wash up on our phones.

CHOPPING ONIONS

Chopping onions
   on a Wednesday night—
   how strange the things
   we remember,
   when our world
   is falling apart,
   disintegrating—
   in slow motion.

I'm not sure
   who cried the most,
   impossible to tell
   when tears hide
   behind tears.

Not that it matters,
   when a bottle
   is empty,
   the wine finished—
   and so are we.

LITTLE DID I KNOW

Little did I know
    how much you
    meant to me—
    my regret,
    the bitter aftertaste
    of hindsight,
    walking alone
    without the hand
    that held my life
    together.

Sunrise

A leg outstretched, the gentle stirring of crisp white sheets, a brilliant sliver of orange glow peeking through the bedroom window.

Pretty lips waking, a soft sigh lost to forest birdsong.

I could watch a million sunrises and still never see one quite as beautiful as your eyes slowly opening in the morning.

Lips

Kisses dream of lips like yours.

My Grandmother

You had already gone before you left this earth. Just a trace of you remained in those final days. A faint voice on the end of a phone, a sudden glimmer of recognition, only to be forgotten in the same breath. My heart breaking as I realized we would never speak again of *Dr. Who*—the sun quickly setting on all those apple pie days.

It's the happy memories I hang on to now. And when I squeeze my eyes shut, I can still see you smiling at me. Hair neatly done. Makeup applied with care. The twinkle in your eye when you laughed at one of my silly stories.

I know, deep down, that's exactly how you would want me to remember you.

The love we had, a bond so strong that not even death could take it away.

Your passing from this world reminded me that we are all just dominoes. Lined up in a neat little row on life's kitchen table. Waiting for our time to fall.

And when my turn comes, I know you will be there, ready to catch me.

A Secret Place

I can take you to a secret place, somewhere not far from here,
where the desert stars sing lullabies to the brokenhearted.

CAN YOU REMEMBER?

I think you loved me,
    the night we drank
    Turkish coffees,
    our fingers woven
    tighter than two
    hands held
    by lovers dangling
    on a precipice
    of a cliff.

Can you remember
    the moment
    our fingers let go?

The stars rushing
    backward,
    no hope left
    below.

NEVER US

It was always about you. Seldom me. And never us.

You Moved On

You moved on—
    before the dust could settle.

So fast—
    not even a single strand
    of silver cobweb
    was left behind
    to hold on to.

No spider could spin
    a web that quickly.

ONLY ONE

When I walk along this lonely path to nowhere—the winter sun speaks to me. In the language of elongated shadows. Now I can only see one, where two once stood.

A Single Kiss

Just when I thought I understood love, all that it could possibly be, you came along and explained its true meaning with a single kiss.

STILLNESS

There is a certain stillness, when even the gentle flutter of a butterfly's wing feels like a hurricane.

The moment when crashing waves fall asleep, peaceful, lost to the serenity of salty dreams.

When tall trees stand to attention and every leaf pauses, takes a deep breath, and holds it.

It is here, beneath the maddening silence, I hear your name.

An echo of you.

FAITH

Love is a little like religion. You need to have faith before miracles can happen.

OUR FIRST BREATH

When we enter this world,
    knowing nothing of life,
    how ironic—
    our first breath
    begins with tears.

Sleepwalking

Lucy pulled up the creaky wooden blinds and peered out the rain-streaked windows.

It was a strange kind of morning.

Wispy gray clouds hung low over the old abandoned church. A sprinkling of watery sunshine touched the treetops of a little park across the road, and in the distance a gorgeous rainbow held the city rooftops in one hand and sparkling sea in the other.

She caught a casual glimpse of herself reflected in the glass.

Strands of straw-colored hair falling across her face, tickling her lips, and almost hiding her sleepwalking eyes.

A trembling hand reached into the pocket of the heavy white dressing gown, searching for the cigarette she had long given up.

"Old habits die hard, and new ones take their place."

Something her shrink had told her at their last session.

She popped the pill into her mouth and walked over to the kitchen counter. Turned on the cold water tap and leaned her head over the sink.

It would be awhile before the Ambien kicked in and heavy legs walked her slowly back to bed.

Just enough time to flip open the laptop, quickly check some e-mails, scroll through her social media, or maybe watch some porn clips and masturbate.

Flopping onto the couch, Lucy switched on the Mac and waited for the all-too-familiar windows to open.

A couple of cute cats, One Direction gif, a woman in pigtails being roughly spanked, and an F. Scott Fitzgerald quote rolled up across the dashboard.

Her fingers came to life, playing a concerto of hearts and reblog clicks, scrolling endlessly past image after image, until she stopped on a video that caught her twitching eye.

It was a homemade porn clip.

A girl in a yellow bikini was slumped down in the passenger seat of a car, baseball cap pulled down over her face. She was furiously rubbing herself, moaning, while the driver, a male arm to be precise, reached over and slid his hand under her top.

Lucy watched and slid a hand beneath her dressing gown.

The girl in the clip pulled her bikini bottom to one side, exposing her shaved pussy, and started to slide her fingers in and out. Her head leaned back into the tan leather seat as she started to moan softly. The familiar tingling and wetness started to tease and tantalize Lucy.

She quickly closed the laptop with one hand while the other hand kept busy. Closing her eyes, she lay down on her back, spreading her long legs a little, kicking a pillow off the couch.

Her mind slipped backward into a world of fleeting fantasies.

A shadowy figure pushed her knees apart and pressed his lips between her legs. While another stood over her, holding his hard cock to her mouth, pushing it in, fucking her open lips.

She cried out as the orgasm hit hard and fast.

Making her sit upright, fingers rubbing her swollen clit, hanging on to the last ripples of spasming pleasure that ran wild through her tense body.

Minutes passed before she could even begin to move.

When she did, each step took its toll, as heavy legs waded through the quicksand of Ambien-induced stupor.

The dressing gown fell silently to the floor, forming a puddle of white on the purple carpet.

Lucy leaned against the windowpane, eyelids heavy, opening and shutting like the graffiti-covered roller doors of a liquor store in a bad neighborhood.

It had stopped raining, and the rainbow was a faded memory lost to bright sunshine.

She could feel the warmth of the glass pressed up against her naked body. It felt comforting. Like a hug from a long-lost lover or a cat curled up under the covers of a bed.

"Old habits die hard, and new ones take their place."

The words did a slow waltz, around and around the empty dance floor, as the darkness descended deep inside her head.

Lucy tumbled down the rabbit hole again.

Where Wonderland ceased to exist.

—

"Will you miss me when I'm gone?" he said.

"I will miss me," she replied.

Open Invitation

You have such a pretty mouth.
 To feed it only kisses
 would be a wasted opportunity.

Saint-Germain

God is in the details,
  you always said.

A blue angel
  dancing on my
  shot glass.

Knocking back
  a flaming sambuca
  at 7:07 a.m.

Sprinkling caviar
  on poached eggs—
  tiny black pearls
  of salty heaven.

A Calum Hood
  bass riff—
  on my headphones.

Writing poetry
  in a hotel room
  in Paris.

Paradise—
  gift wrapped
  on a Sunday morning.

THE CONVERSATION

Let's continue this conversation in bed, she whispered.
My legs can't wait to hear what your hands have to say.

FINGERS BURNT

A bad relationship can be defined by the striking of a match. The longer you hold on to it, the greater the likelihood of getting your fingers burnt.

WITH YOU

Whenever I'm with you,
   the clocks stop ticking,
   death is forgotten,
   and spilt milk—
   stays spilt.

Time Travelers

Drinking Tito's vodka
    at the café by the beach.

The roar of distant waves
    breaking the silence.

Closing the space
    between this reality
    and the past.

A gust of wind
    running its fingers
    through your hair.

Our secret revealed
    while you scan
    the winter menu.

My pencil glued
    to a crossword puzzle,
    stuck on 7 down.

Kissing—
    is the missing word
    you suggest.

Your regret sparkling
    in summer eyes.

Remembering—
another time,
in a different place.

Before we became
just friends.

Without the benefits.

HIDE-AND-SEEK

There were days when it seemed like I was trapped in an endless game of hide-and-seek with myself.

RACISM

Racism is the hate child of ignorance and arrogance.

IMPERFECTION

I have always found beauty in the crooked and flawed.

A lone dark cloud dancing on a stage of brilliant blue. The honesty of a song sung slightly out of tune. A pretty pink scar, its story told in a sentence written on a milky white thigh.

I think that's why I love you and all your little eccentricities.

The exquisite poetry of imperfection.

Beautifully broken and wonderfully damaged.

BOOK

Put your hands on my knees, she said, and think of me as a book you've been dying to read.

We Didn't Fall in Love

We didn't fall in love—
    it was more like
    the slow descent
    of a feather
    on a windless day.

A leaky tap
    filling an ocean,
    drip by drip.

Like our world
    had forgotten
    how to turn.

In a universe
    high on morphine.

You Are Beautiful

The one thing we all have in common is our differences. Embrace your uniqueness. You are beautiful just the way you are.

A MUSE

She was a muse
    cursed with melancholia,
    her tears the ink
    on my typewriter ribbon.

The Kitty Club

I'm not sure whose idea it was, but it all seemed to make sense at the bottom of a vodka bottle.

Sophia tripping over the cat, correcting herself with her bare arms outstretched, walking over to the fridge on tiptoes. A tipsy girl in floral panties, smudged red lipstick, and messy hair.

All I can remember, through the haze of slurred words and the chinking of shot glasses, was that the sex had been amazing.

"You're out of milk," she shouted. Hanging off the fridge door like a sheet that had lost one peg on a clothesline.

"There's some ice cream in the freezer. Maybe you can use that."

"I'm okay with black anyway; the stronger the coffee, the better," Sophia replied.

Well, I think that's how the conversation went.

—

The new morning streamed through my bedroom window, waking me in the worst possible way.

A dazzling beam of bright sunlight blinding my squinting eyes, and my head pounding.

I sat up out of bed, hovered for a matter of seconds, before collapsing back onto the pillows.

Sophia danced into the bedroom, headphones on, and threw a bottle of water onto the bed. She flashed me a smile, did a little shimmy, and danced out of the room.

She was wearing one of my shirts and nothing else.

I felt a familiar stirring under the sheet.

A hangover hard-on.

I reached for the bottle of water and cursed my stupidity for falling into the vodka trap. By now I should have known better than to try to keep up with her. I always paid a shocking price.

"You should think about hopping into the shower."

Sophia's shouted command from the lounge made me wince as a foggy memory descended over my fuzzy brain.

I closed my eyes and visualized the promise I had made the night before.

Now I remembered.

It had been my idea to take Sophia to the Kitty Club for lunch.

What the hell had I been thinking?

—

The codeine had finally kicked in, and I started to feel human again.

Sitting in the white leather back seat of Sophia's silver Bentley, driven by her pretty assistant, Marie.

My head propped up against the window watching the trees whizz by.

Sophia had arranged the ride while I was drowning in the shower, the cold water slapping my body back to life.

Marie had also brought over a change of clothes for her.

"What do you think? Skirt short enough?"

I turned and gazed at Sophia's outfit.

The gray woolen pleated skirt riding up, giving a flash of red satin panties, her long black-stockinged legs attached to a pair of pale pink stripper heels.

Her look neatly finished off with a tight, body-hugging, buttoned white blouse.

"I think if you're going for kinky secretary chic, you've surpassed yourself."

"Funny man. Let's see who has the last laugh when we get to the club."

I'd almost forgotten about why we were hurtling along the backcountry road.

My dumb idea.

I had never been to the Kitty Club but heard they served up a fabulous seafood lunch and swinging sex as dessert.

There had been a write-up about the place in *Outrageous* magazine, and Sophia was all-in when I casually mentioned it to her in between shots of vodka.

Marie hit the horn.

A group of ducks flew up from the road, narrowly missing the windshield.

She then spun the wheel, doing a hand brake turn, sliding the Bentley into a tight left-hand corner.

"Fuck! What the fuck!" I yelled, my head slamming back into the headrest.

Sophia grinned and patted my leg.

"Look, we're almost there," said Marie, laughing.

The Bentley slowed down to an elegant purr as it rolled up the gravel driveway, a row of conifer trees lining the sides.

I could see a sandstone manor perched on a hill in the near distance.

"It looks so gorgeous," Sophia sighed.

—

We were met at the steps by two gentlemen dressed in identical white tuxedos and dark sunglasses.

One of them took the keys from Marie, and the other handed us each a narrow black velvet mask.

"Discretion is everything," he said politely as the three of us put on the masks.

We looked like well-dressed cat burglars.

"Now just take the steps up to the main door and please wait to be seated."

Sophia took a £50 note from her Prada handbag and tried to give the tip to the attendant.

He waved his hand and smiled.

"No need," he said. "It's our pleasure to have you as our guests."

We walked up the steps and pushed open the heavy wooden door that led to a grand marble hallway and antique reception desk, where we were greeted by a well-dressed elderly woman who looked like she had stepped out of a classic black-and-white 1940s Hollywood movie.

"Welcome to the Kitty Club!" she said warmly. "Now before I take you to your table, I just want to tell you about the house rules. First, treat everyone with respect, and remember no means no. Secondly, the club has the right to remove any guest who is rude or gets drunk. The third rule is terribly important; all gentlemen must wear a condom when performing. Lastly, have fun, my dears!"

Sophia leaned over and whispered into my ear. "I hope you paid close attention to the second rule."

"My name is Edna, and if you need anything or have any questions, please just ask one of our waiters. If you'd be so very kind to settle your account now, it makes everything so much easier."

Sophia handed over her black Amex card to Edna, who swiped it and handed it back along with a small green velvet bag.

"Just a few things you might need for later," she said with a cheeky smile.

—

We were seated in the grand dining room by our waitress, Penelope, a stunning blonde dressed in a neatly pressed French maid's outfit.

The table was covered by a pristine white tablecloth, with silver cutlery and white bone china plates sitting perfectly upon it.

A vase of red roses placed in the middle.

I sat down and scanned the room, trying not to look too obvious.

The other guests all wore the same masks and were immaculately dressed. Deep in conversation and it seemed like a mixture of ages.

Penelope handed us each a brown leather-bound menu with the words "Kitty Club" embossed on the front.

"As you can see, today we are serving our famous seafood selection platter, with a choice of three vintage champagnes. If you are a vegan, our chef is also serving a gorgeous wild mushroom lasagna with shaved white truffles and garden-picked asparagus, lemon-infused olive oil, and roasted almonds."

Marie's face lit up, and she could hardly contain her smile.

"Well, that's me decided. I'll definitely be having the lasagna."

Sophia looked over at me.

"Guess we'll be sharing the platter, then. What do you fancy for the selection?"

I scanned the menu.

There was a long list of delicious seafood to choose from, and I could already feel my mouth salivating at the prospect of sampling the cuisine.

"I think the orange butter grilled lobsters are a must, two dozen of the natural oysters, sea urchin, the chili soft shell crab, and the vodka salmon gravlax sounds good too."

Penelope scribbled on her notepad with a pencil.

"And a side order of the black caviar and parmesan hand-cut fries would be great," added Sophia.

"Excellent!" replied Penelope. "May I also suggest a bottle of the Krug '89 to get you started?"

"Wonderful! I can't wait." Sophia gave Penelope a sly wink.

Our waitress slid away, and Marie opened the bag Edna had given us. She comically held her hands to her mouth in shock. Inside were a couple of tubes of lube and several condom packets.

I laughed.

Sophia giggled.

It was going to be an interesting lunch.

—

The food was magnificent.

After finishing off our second bottle of champagne, we were led away from our table by Penelope, up a spiral staircase to "our bedroom." Most of the other guests had already left the dining room.

"You'll find some toiletries, toothbrushes, and toothpaste in the bathroom. Please take a shower, and when you're done, enter the gold doorway at the end of the hall. You can hang your clothes in the wardrobe, and there is a safe for your valuables too. Not that we have ever had anything stolen. You'll find dressing gowns in the wardrobe, all sizes, no need to wear anything underneath, and don't forget to take your green bag with you. Do you have any questions?"

Sophia smiled and lightly tapped Penelope's shoulder with her hand.

"Any chance you'll be joining the party later?"

Penelope grinned. "You just never know."

Our waitress walked out of the bedroom and closed the door with a quiet click.

"Oh my, check this out," called Marie from the bathroom.

Sophia and I entered the palatial en suite bathroom. It became instantly obvious what had caught Marie's attention. The shower cubicle was huge, with multiple showerheads.

"Room for all of us," Sophia chuckled.

"Why don't you girls go first? I'm going to take a look at those robes."

"You're such a bloody prude, seriously! Where is your sense of adventure? Look, Marie is game."

I ignored Sophia's teasing jibe and tried not to look at Marie as she unzipped the black dress she was wearing, letting it fall to the red-and-black-tiled floor. Closely followed by a matching black bra and panties.

"I thought you were leaving, you pervert," laughed Sophia.

I left the two girls to it and returned to the bedroom. Opening the wardrobe, I saw the collection of robes hanging inside. They were all made of red silk, and I took one off the coat hanger.

I laid the robe onto the king-size bed and noticed a minibar tucked neatly away in the corner.

Opening the minibar fridge, I found it stocked with rows and rows of little bottles of spirits. I reached in and took a bottle of Grey Goose vodka, unscrewed the cap, and swallowed the contents in one gulp.

It was then that I heard the loud moaning coming from the bathroom. Not even the hiss of the showerheads could disguise it.

Little did I know then, this would be nothing compared to what would happen next.

—

The gold door at the end of the hallway opened onto what could best be described as a ballroom. Except nobody was dancing beneath the dimly lit chandeliers.

Wherever I looked, couples and groups of masked naked bodies were engaged in all manner of sexual acts. On tables, leather couches, against the walls, and even on the emerald green carpet that covered the entire floor.

A young man with a massive erection walked over to us. He was wearing a white-colored mask.

"Welcome to the orgy room. My name is Jackson, and I'm one of the hosts. I can take your robes."

Sophia whispered in my ear. "Feeling a bit inadequate, are we?"

I gently pushed her away and removed my robe and handed it to Jackson.

"There you go," I said in my most cavalier voice.

My frequent visits to the beaches in the South of France had prepared me well for public nudity.

Marie and Sophia handed over their robes next.

"Now how many of these do you think you'll need?" said Marie, taking three condom packets from the bag we had been given and holding them up in her petite hand.

I took one.

Jackson laughed. "Oh, I think you'll be needing more than that."

Sophia reached over and started rubbing my flaccid cock.

I felt my cheeks flush red with embarrassment. Which given the activity in the room did make me feel a little prudish.

It was like Jackson could read my mind, and he quickly tried to put it at rest.

"Everyone has the first-time jitters, but believe me, just relax and go with it."

Marie must have already taken his advice to heart.

She dropped to her knees and performed her infamous party trick. Sliding a condom onto Jackson's hard cock with her mouth. He let out a deep groan as her pretty red lips covered the tip of his huge shaft.

I must admit her spontaneous act made my cock swell and stand to attention.

"Come on, let's go fuck," cooed Sophia, taking me by the hand and leading me over to a corner of the giant room.

I sat down on a large brown leather-studded chair and slid on a condom. Sophia straddled me, guiding my hard cock into her tight, wet pussy.

We started to fuck, and it felt amazing. Maybe it was the sight of all the others doing it and the sounds of the orgy echoing throughout the ballroom that made the sex feel so hot.

A girl with blond hair leaned in between us. Despite her wearing a white mask, I could tell it was our waitress from the dining room. She locked lips with Sophia, who reached down between Penelope's long legs and started rubbing her shaved pussy.

This just turned me on even more, and I gripped Sophia's slender waist and fucked her harder, faster, and deeper.

When the orgasm hit, it did so with an intensity that made my whole body shudder.

Sophia hopped off me and laid down on the carpet, legs spread, while Penelope gently sucked on her swollen pink clitoris.

Jackson was right.

I certainly would need more than one condom to survive this debauched afternoon gathering.

—

The drive home was a sedate one.

We were so exhausted we hardly even noticed how beautiful the sunset was outside the windows of the Bentley.

Sophia was the first to break the silence. "Well, that was fun."

Always the champion of the understatement.

We all burst out laughing.

Marie looked into the rearview mirror.

"I thought the lasagna was one of the best things I've ever eaten."

"Second only to Jackson's cock," Sophia replied, grinning.

"Well, I'm pleased you both enjoyed your lunch at the Kitty Club, one of my better ideas, I think," I said smugly.

Sophia pinched my arm with a mock expression of surprise on her beautiful face.

"Your idea? I distinctly remember it was me who suggested we go last night. Honestly, after a few vodkas you'd forget your head was attached to your neck."

I knew better than to get into a debate with Sophia.

—

A full moon was peeking slowly above the crooked rooftops of the tired terrace houses.

Loved-up couples, walking hand in hand, weaved their way along the narrow streets of Soho, stepping around the groups of drunk revelers looking for their next drink.

Marie pulled the Bentley up outside the glass doors of the Purple Palace, a small boutique hotel where Sophia stayed whenever she was in London.

"Would you like to come inside for a quick martini?"

Sophia saw the hesitation in my eyes. There was never such a thing as a quick martini or anything when it came to this girl.

"Or I can get Marie to run you back home?" she quickly added with a flutter of her gorgeous eyelashes.

She was the abridged version of all the love letters I had ever written. Beautifully concise and impossible to resist.

It was going to be another long night.

GRATITUDE

Take nothing for granted. Even a rock will eventually surrender to the sea, and love can slip away like sand through fingers.

INTO DEPTHS

Into depths of ocean blue—
    your summer eyes
    reflect in mine,
    your smile,
    a rousing,
    rising sun—
    greets a morning
    made for two.

We swim,
    my love—
    beneath a sea
    billowing white,
    upon a bed
    of coral pink,
    against the muted
    light of dawn,
    sun-kissed bodies
    gently sink.

Inside Every Cherry

In matters of love it's tempting to be picky. But never forget, inside every cherry, no matter how delicious—you'll always find a stone.

THE YEAR OF THE RAT

2020—I have never experienced a year like it. Bad news followed by worse. It felt like I was living in a house of cards. Waiting for the next hurricane to hit.

SUMMER

It was like you held a tiny glowing sun in the palm of your hand. Your delicate fingers—rays of golden light. Each gentle touch—a warm breeze caressing my skin.

Reminding me of every summer I had ever known.

Ruin Me

"I'm the kind of girl who has a restless mind and impatient legs . . ."

I watched as her fingers nervously flicked the well-worn elastic of her white cotton panties.

"I want you to ruin me."

MELTING ICE CREAM

"You seem restless tonight," I said, as we sat down for dessert.

"Oh, it's nothing really. It'll pass. Just pour me another glass of wine," she replied with a wry smile. "But if you're really concerned for my well-being—lift up my skirt, bend me over this table, and fuck me until the ice cream melts."

PERHAPS

The inability to be decisive—
    to ponder love
    with no conclusion,
    to give hope
    when all is hopeless,
    there is no divide
    more divisive.

Stars

Magic tumbled from her pretty lips, and when she spoke the language of the universe—the stars sighed in unison.

ALONE AGAIN

There are those
    who walk,
    the lucky ones run,
    and then there's us—
    the unfortunate few,
    who stumble
    at the first hurdle,
    always left behind
    in this wretched race
    others call love.

Respect

So she gave
    you a smile,
    but that's no excuse
    to justify
    your unwanted
    attention.

It's just an illusion,
    your fucked-up delusion,
    not a permission
    to take her to bed.

It's time
    to respect,
    instead of expect,
    to acknowledge
    the wrongs
    of the past.

And when she
    says no,
    you know it
    means no,
    and just once
    it needs only
    be said.

DESIRE

I never understood desire until I felt your hands around my throat.

Awake

I became so obsessed with you that I even convinced myself that you loved me.

SOPHIA

What do you want to do today?

It was one of those questions you dread, especially after an evening spent destroying a damn good bottle of Russian vodka and waking with a hangover that could demolish a large building.

I took another look at the text with blurry morning eyes and decided to play dead for a few minutes longer before responding.

No such luck as the next text pinged on my phone.

??????????????????

Sophia wasn't the kind of girl to let sleeping dogs lie or have texts go unanswered.

Lunch, The Gallery, 12:30?

It was the best my trembling fingers could think of for a reply, and perhaps a couple of coffee martinis might be the fix my fuzzy brain desperately needed.

Sophia's reply came lightning fast.

Yes!!!!!!!!!!!!!!

———

I arrived at the restaurant like a man walking through thick mud.

The steaming hot shower and Red Bull had helped, but only just. Sophia was sitting at our favorite table in the corner, head down and scanning the menu.

"Sorry I'm late," I said, collapsing into the chair and summoning over a waiter.

"I hope it was a pleasant death," Sophia laughed, eyes locked on mine.

The Gallery was a darling of a restaurant. Small, cozy, and unassuming, apart from the million-dollar paintings hanging on the cream-colored walls. The restaurant was the indulgent hobby of the owner, Malcolm Devlin, who had made his fortune as a Wall Street trader before relocating to London to pursue his hospitality ambitions. There were no reservations or casual walk-ins allowed. It was a membership-only affair, with guests carefully vetted and an annual fee paid that covered all the exquisite food and fine wines. A little like a timeshare arrangement. Sophia's brushed metal card gave her entry for Wednesday lunch times and the coveted Saturday nights.

A coffee martini was placed quietly next to me while Sophia rattled off the order for both of us. Two dozen oysters to start, followed by the seafood platter for two and a bottle of Taittinger champagne on the side. The immaculately groomed waiter flashed her a smile and took the menu away.

"I thought I'd best handle the important decisions for the day," she smiled, leaning over and kissing me on the cheek.

I loved this gorgeous girl who had the delightful habit of drifting into my life at the most unexpected moments. Wild and unpredictable, ridiculously rich and with a heart of gold to match. The last time we had met was six months ago at Sophia's 30th, a dinner party that started with a birthday card and ended up in the tabloids. Celebrities and paparazzi fighting on the sidewalk.

"So how long are you in town?" I asked. "You know, it would have been nice to have had some warning. I would have gone easy last night and feel much better for it."

"Drink up," she replied. "You'll be right in no time."

I drained the last drop from the martini glass, only to have it instantly replaced by the grinning waiter. Sophia was intent on getting me pleasantly plastered it seemed. Which was always her motivation whenever we met.

"So come on, tell me, how long are you here for this time?" I asked again.

"Just the one night, on the red-eye tomorrow morning, heading off to Paris and then Milan," she replied.

The oysters arrived on a plate of crushed ice, seaweed, and sliced organic lemons.

"They're all for you," she smiled, reaching for a glass of freshly poured champagne. "Did you think I would buy you lunch without some pretty strings attached?"

The coffee martinis had kicked in and I could feel a mischievous smile writing itself across my tired face. "So you booked a room for later too," I said, laughing.

Whenever we met in London it always ended up beneath the silk sheets of a messy bed in the Purple Palace, a small boutique hotel in Soho. Where discretion was served up nightly along with Belgian chocolates and a bouquet of bloodred roses. I loved the place, and so did Sophia.

It was going to be a quick lunch.

—

"Untie me, please."

Sophia looked up, her green eyes sparkling in the candlelight.

Wrists tied to the bedposts by sheer black stockings and a just-fucked wetness between her legs.

I did as I was told, my eyes never leaving hers, as I gently liberated each outstretched arm.

"We really should get married," I said, sitting down on the edge of the bed.

"Ha! Now wouldn't that be a hoot," she laughed. "The magazines would love it. However, I'm not sure Serena would be too thrilled with that arrangement. No, I think things are just perfect as they are, silly boy."

Serena was Sophia's longtime partner. Both enjoyed an open relationship and tolerated each other's little discretions, as long as they didn't get too serious. More to the point, I really got on well with Serena and loved the nights we all spent together, drinking too much red wine and solving the problems of the world over a candlelit dinner table.

"I was joking."

Sophia sighed. "Really?"

It was a subtle hint of repressed regret that escaped her pretty lips and a deep-down sadness I shared too, every time she walked out of my life.

I felt her arms wrap around me, pulling my body closer to hers as we fell into an embrace that seemed to stop all time in its tracks.

It was love, and neither of us could deny it.

—

Returning home in the taxi, I found myself staring blankly out of the window, taking in the early morning pantomime of sleepy pedestrians waking up to the prospect of another working day. Faces painted with grim expressions and heads buried in iPhones.

My mind drifted away to that magical moment when Sophia and I met for the first time at a garden party.

Both of us tipsy, doing a clumsy waltz around the circular dance floor, trying our best not to bump into the other guests but failing spectacularly.

Her head resting on my shoulder, the chemistry between us instant and intoxicating.

When the music stopped, Sophia smiled and looked into my eyes with an intensity that ignited a fire deep within my heart.

I can still remember the first words she spoke.

"I'm not the kind of girl who wants her name tattooed on your arm," *she purred. "Think of me as your dirty little secret."*

MASS DELUSION

Melting ice caps
    and burning trees,
    dolphins strangled
    in plastic seas,
    temperatures rising
    by alarming degrees,
    poisoned rivers
    and dying bees,
    a crying world
    brought to its knees.

But don't panic—
    Instagram's back up.

Waiting for Monday

Never on a Sunday,
    you once said.

The day of rest
    for restless legs,
    and praying hands
    that beg for sex.

Promises kept—
    with playful eyes.

Fingers counting
    down the hours
    on open thighs.

Waiting for Monday
    to come.

Run

When you know you're in a toxic relationship don't just walk away. Run.

SECOND CHANCE

We kissed beneath the twisted trees,
    our lips between the stars,
    tiny ripples in a lake,
    this love, once lost,
    is ours.

Conflicting Emotions

Just when you think you can't love someone more than you already do—your heart skips a beat and reminds your brain just how wrong it is.

FOREPLAY

Your words touch me in a way I find difficult to describe, she said, although whenever I read them it feels a lot like foreplay.

How Strange

How strange these late nights—dreaming of sleep. Listening to the owls sing and thinking about you.

Midnight in Manhattan

A quiet sigh escaped from scarlet lips.

Sophia loved the caress of lingerie on her skin—the secret thrill of hard nipples pressed against black lace.

Her reflection a ghost in the moonlight, haunting a rain-streaked hotel window.

—

Sophia turned around and smiled.

She watched as Serena unzipped her tight red leather dress and let it fall to the floor.

"You seem happy to be back in the city."

"I am. Very much so," Sophia replied, walking slowly over to Serena and kissing her hard on the lips.

Serena slid a hand between Sophia's long legs, feeling the wetness beneath her pretty panties.

Sophia sighed again.

—

"I love New York. The perfect place to read books, people watch, and fuck to the sound of sirens screaming late at night."

WHEN THE ROMANCE GOES

I remember a time when you made me daisy chains.
Now you just mow the lawn.

CAROUSEL

The relationship was going nowhere, but that's what I loved about it. Uncomplicated and predictable. Like riding on a beautiful carousel with a pocketful of coins.

THE STAIRCASE

When it comes to finding true love, some people just get lucky. The elevator doors magically open, and they get an easy ride to the top. The rest of us have to take the fucking staircase. One miserable step at a time.

Words

Words are powerful things. They can break hearts and make panties wet.

STAY TOGETHER

Never say never
    nor question whether,
    two distant hearts
    can stay together,
    for true love
    is a ship
    that can sail
    in any weather.

The Mermaid

She came from the ocean,
    this wild girl from the sea,
    her hair flowing southward,
    she walked toward me.

A west to east smile,
    with eyes steely gray,
    like a storm in the distance,
    rolling in from the bay.

We kissed with the sunrise,
    made love when it set,
    a promise by moonlight,
    came dawn, my regret.

He left for the ocean,
    this boy from the land,
    his spirit soars northward,
    his heart in her hands.

Chasing Love

When chasing love
   at any cost—

The pathways meet
   but seldom cross.

I dream of dreams—

Once dreamt,
   now lost.

How sunshine steals
   from autumn frost.

The Wedding Present

The big day had finally arrived, and it was chaos. Mandy was beside herself, rearranging the flowers for the fifth time, placing long-stemmed white tulips into vases scattered around the bedroom. All the guests would be arriving any minute now, and she hadn't even sorted the bottles of champagne and glasses. Rupert watched her race around the room in the reflection of the wardrobe mirror, a smile breaking across his cleanly shaved face as his fingers wrestled with the white bowtie.

"Oh here, let me do that," said Simon as he waltzed into the room wearing a white tuxedo, looking like a million dollars. He quickly took control of Rupert's bowtie drama and tied it perfectly in less than ten seconds.

Rupert kissed him on the cheek. "What would I do without you? How do I look?"

Simon gave him a quick look up and down. Rupert was wearing a matching white tuxedo but with a scarlet handkerchief tucked into the top pocket of his jacket. "You are the best-looking husband this side of the river."

"Not yet," Rupert replied, grinning.

"And bloody never at this rate!" Mandy screamed. "Come on, you two, sort yourselves out. We have a wedding to get done."

The doorbell rang.

Mandy started to panic again.

—

It was Rupert's idea to exchange vows in bed. He was a big John Lennon fan and wanted to channel John and Yoko's famous 1969 "bed-ins for peace" vibe. Simon loved the idea, too, but only if it was just for one day and not a whole week, he had repeatedly stressed to a bemused Rupert.

The ceremony had gone smoothly. Simon's sister, Mandy, presided over the exchange of vows. She was a part-time marriage celebrant and wedding planner. Even the Skype call from Simon and Mandy's parents had gone off without a hitch. Wishing the happy couple all the very best from the cabin of their cruise ship sailing in the Mediterranean. The wedding had been a spur-of-the-moment decision, another of Rupert's bright ideas, so there was no way they could get back for it in time.

When the happy couple exchanged identical gold rings and kissed for the first time as husband and husband, the bedroom erupted with cheers and loud applause. The love so powerful in the room, barely a dry eye could be seen on any of the guests.

And now that the official part was done and dusted, the party was in full swing.

Twelve of their dearest and closest friends knocked back the champagne, cracked jokes, and chatted with the happy couple lying in their huge bed, propped up on pillows, a pile of neatly wrapped wedding presents sitting on a side table. ABBA's

"I Do, I Do, I Do, I Do, I Do" blaring out of the Bose speakers.

Mandy topped up Simon's glass with more champagne, and he caught the worried expression on her face. He knew what was wrong. Not everything had gone to plan. But before he could say anything, she quickly walked off, checking her watch repeatedly.

The doorbell rang.

"I'll get it!" Mandy shouted, running out of the bedroom in a flash.

———

Rupert was halfway through telling a particularly filthy joke when Mandy poked her head around the bedroom door and caught his eye with a wave of her hand. He stopped short of the punchline and called out to her.

"What is it, darling?" he shouted over the music.

Mandy hit a button on a remote and the music stopped. Everyone turned in her direction.

"Rupert, you have a special delivery. It's in the living room," she said nervously.

"Well, well, well, what could it be?" Rupert replied excitedly, as he hopped out of bed. "You coming, husband, to have a peek?"

Simon gave Mandy a quick glance. She nodded back. "No, I'll wait here. You go. I'll keep the bed warm."

Rupert giggled and took Mandy by the hand. "Come on, love, let's go see what all this fuss is about."

—

In an instant, the blood literally drained from Rupert's face. His smile wiped clean.

"What the fuck are you doing here?" he said angrily.

Mandy gently squeezed his hand. "Just listen to what he has to say."

Standing in the living room was a tall, elderly man dressed in a gray suit, yellow tie, and neatly polished black shoes. A white ribbon had been tied around his waist, complete with an oversized bow. He looked Rupert in the eyes and spoke. His voice already starting to break.

"Hi, Son. Sorry I'm late. Plane was delayed . . ."

Rupert cut him off. "Fuck your excuses. I don't care. Just get the fuck out of my house!"

The old man stood up straight, took a deep breath, and continued talking.

"Son, I will go. But not before I say something I should have said to you years ago. I'm so sorry. Sorry for how I've treated you in the past. Sorry for my ignorance. I'm ashamed. Deeply ashamed, for not accepting you for who you are. I was wrong to turn my back on you. When we lost your mother, my world collapsed, and when you told me you were gay, it felt like I had lost you too. It was all me, never you. It's my fault our relationship broke down. The blame rests with me, and I wish I could turn back the clock. I honestly do. I'm not asking for your forgiveness, and I don't want to spoil your big day. But when Simon tracked me down and rang me, when he told me you were getting married, my heart sank. Made me realize what a fool I've been. How much time we have lost because of me. I never stopped loving you, Son, and I wanted you to know that. Anyway, I'll leave you be now, get on my way."

Rupert said nothing and just watched silently as his dad tried to undo the white ribbon Mandy had wrapped around him. His arthritic fingers shaking as they tugged at the bow. Rupert could see the tears welling up in his father's tired eyes.

"Let me do that," said Mandy in a quiet voice.

"No. I'll do it," Rupert said as he walked over to his dad and hugged him. The old man bursting into tears, sobbing uncontrollably into his son's shoulder. Rupert patted his back. "Hush now. You'll ruin this bloody tux, and it cost a fortune."

The old man looked up. A faint smile appearing on his wrinkled face. "Good to see you haven't lost your sense of humor, Son."

"Okay, enough of this," said Rupert, brushing away a tear from his eye. "You'll set me off crying, too, at this rate. And this is a wedding. Not a fucking funeral! Now come on, Dad, it's time you met my fabulous husband."

The old man took a comb from his pocket and ran it through his thinning white hair.

"I'd love to, Son."

After Life

I can still see your face
    in the changing clouds,
    searching for me
    in summer raindrops.

Suddenly—
    two white doves
    land on a single branch.

My morning revelation.

You always said,
    we will be together.

Not even death
    could keep us apart.

In Your Eyes

In your eyes I see myself. I see the love we never thought was possible.

Seduction

The more buttons you undo, she said, the faster I become undone.

Red Cotton Panties

You love to touch yourself with your panties on. Lying next to me in the bed. Your hand under the hem, fingers softly rubbing your clitoris.

A dark wet patch spreading across the cheap red cotton.

I place my hand over yours. So I can feel the movement—the rhythmic circles becoming faster, as you pleasure yourself with eyes closed.

My lips press against your ear and whisper dirty pretty things.

"Does your pussy feel good?"

"Spread your legs a little wider."

"Imagine having a big cock stretching you open—fucking you."

The breathy moans become louder.

Quicker.

When the orgasm finally comes, I pull on your pink nipples with my fingers. Making your hips buck uncontrollably. Legs writhing with every intense wave.

—

A beautiful moment of dreamy calm.

Your pretty face flushed and a quiet smile resting on your lips. I watch as you slide your legs out of the soaking wet panties and reach down for them.

You gaze deeply into my eyes and speak ever so softly.

"How would you like to feel my dirty panties on your hard cock?"

You don't wait for a reply. My eyes close as you wrap them around the shaft of my cock. I feel the damp fabric and your sticky juice on my skin.

Your hand pulls my thick cock up and down.

Harder.

Faster.

Until you feel the familiar throb beneath your delicate fingers. Biting down on your lip while you watch me cum all over your panties.

Hearing me say your name.

Over and over again.

Denial

Do not be fooled by my air of nonchalance, the hesitation in my words, for deep down it is all just a hopeless deception. It is my unbridled fear of rejection that keeps me trapped in this sorry state of denial. Can you see the cracks appearing in this wall I have built? Like a dam dangerously close to bursting— my love a raging torrent waiting to break free.

OUR AUTUMN CAME

Our autumn came
    in coffee cups,
    from clouds of white
    to swirling brown,
    all wrinkly leaf,
    on muddy ground,
    the sugary sweet,
    sipped and stirred,
    with silver spoon
    and parting words,
    a butter knife
    on buttered toast,
    a morning mourned
    with marmalade.

No fond farewell
    in silence made,
    just falling tears
    in fallen rain,
    all sunshine gone
    no warmth remains,
    in empty cups,
    our autumn came.

Sweet Corruption

How wonderful it is to wander in this valley of sweet corruption. Where fingers walk between the banks of a flowing river, and lips taste the nectar of summer peaches, left to ripen in the sun.

I Miss You

My pen knows no limit when it comes to expressing my love for you, but when we're apart, I miss you beyond words.

CHOCOLATE

She was the kind of girl
    who loved to stretch out
    under the sheets,
    eating chocolate,
    reading books—
    and fucking on
    rainy afternoons.

Resentment

Life is a long wooden bridge that spans rushing rivers, steep ravines, and deep canyons. You never know exactly where it will take you or who you will meet along the way. The fastest way to burn it is to let resentment strike the match.

A Broken Pencil

Being told to move on from a relationship is like being asked to draw a smile with a broken pencil.

THE GIFT

Her eyes were beautifully gift-wrapped—long black lashes of velvet ribbon—and every time she opened them, it felt like Christmas.

STANDING ON THE PRECIPICE

Sometimes we encounter a blurred line between right and wrong. The ink smudged by guilt and unbridled ego. We find ourselves conflicted—wondering what to do?

To complicate matters, sometimes a *right* is another person's *wrong*.

And vice versa.

Such is the dilemma of perspectives and differing points of view. When standing on the edge of a precarious moral precipice. Wondering whether to jump or not?

Thinking the worst but hoping for the best—with eyes tightly shut. Realizing you could end up fucked no matter what decision you make.

But knowing that the fear of making a mistake—*is the real mistake*.

The only thing stopping us from flying.

LOVE LETTERS

The kind of love letters I write are the ones you read in bed, stretched out under the sheets with one hand between your legs.

Days Always Pass

Days always pass quicker when happiness keeps time. And just like that—another beautiful day slips silently away.

Truth or Dare?

Truth or dare? How we loved to play that party game as teenagers. No matter which one we chose, it was just all a bit of fun. No serious repercussions. Except perhaps that time when Mark jumped off the shed roof and spent the rest of the summer break with his leg in a cast. Even when Penny admitted she had a crush on her sports teacher—Miss Waddle, I think that was her name—we all just shrugged it off with howls of laughter.

Whatever happened to those innocent times?

When did it all change?

How did we end up here?

Straitlaced and judgmental. Boring adults who bite their lips before speaking. Too afraid to say what we really think and feel. Tiptoeing our way through inane dinner conversations. Playing a brand-new game. Where telling the truth has become the ultimate dare.

DREAMS

She turns her mind
  to countless things,
  then back again
  where it begins.

This restless urge,
  and all it brings,
  to be someone—
  to do something.

TOMORROW

How quickly we forget the sun will rise again tomorrow.

Peace

When others speak of war—it's time to raise our voices and fight for peace.

SUNSETS NEVER LIE

Do you remember that gorgeous spring morning back in 1986? When the joys of youth surged through our bodies as we ran barefoot through Central Park. Holding hands with arms outstretched. Like a supersonic jet racing across a sea of green, powered by love.

How we collapsed by that giant oak tree trying to catch our breath. Faces flushed, eyes shining in the sunlight, hearts beating under our matching "I love New York" tees.

The promise we made after the third kiss.

To live the rest of our lives in this wonderful city.

—

Only the cursed walk outside now. Lost souls in dressing gowns, shuffling past the empty shops with smashed windows, burnt-out cars, and mountains of decaying trash.

The last few New Yorkers who haven't yet developed any symptoms remain barricaded in their dark apartments. Drinking dirty water dripping from taps. Scraping the last bits of food from empty cans or chewing on the bones of a much-loved family pet.

How naive of us to believe things wouldn't get this bad, let alone far worse. Even more devastating than when COVID stalked the world. All those years ago.

Every night, I hear the single gunshots echoing off the skyscrapers. Broken souls self-medicating. Blowing their brains out in white-tiled bathrooms and messy bedrooms.

All power is out—the internet down and the phone system dead.

Not a single government department, business, or even hospital is still functioning.

The last emergency broadcast I heard before the radio went silent was a report that the president had succumbed to *Pandora* and died. Along with seventy other personnel at the bunker facility in Virginia.

There are no more riots, no more looting, no more anything.

Death is running the show now.

—

I wish I could turn back the clock and relive all the happy times we spent together.

Snuggling up on the sofa watching Netflix.

Smoking joints and bursting out laughing as we lost the plot playing Scrabble.

You singing '80s songs into your wine glass, while I made dumplings in the kitchen.

Innocents believing this would be our life forever.

Now I just wish I could tell you, one last time—how much I love you.

—

My fingers are struggling to keep pushing this tired pencil.

The last letter I will ever write.

Thankfully, the time has come for me to escape this overwhelming pain. The tragedy of love and unfathomable loss.

But not before I take one final glimpse of late afternoon beauty.

A golden glow of orange streaming through the lounge-room window. Framing your sleeping body stretched out on the sofa. One arm hanging over the edge—fingers resting on the carpet. Sparkles of light, like tiny diamonds, dancing on a dropped whiskey glass. Sleeping pills spilt and scattered.

The wonderful serenity of a silent heart magnified in my teardrop.

Sunsets never lie.

Rage Against Love

Spare me your pity—
    the worthless platitudes,
    just let me rage
    against love.

Set my heart free—
    just leave me be,
    to rip the stars
    from the night sky,
    while I scream—
    go fuck yourself
    to the moon.

Please—
    pretty please,
    just let me rage
    against love.

Who Am I?

We live so many lives in a single lifetime that it is often difficult to reconcile the person we once were with the stranger staring back at us in the mirror.

PLEASE STAY

Please stay,
    just a little longer,
    let not the ticking
    of a clock
    force our arms apart,
    for time loses meaning,
    becomes nothing—
    without you.

Last Summer

Her skin was the color of burnt caramel, so beautiful and almost glowing in the dying rays of a sleepy sun. Brown eyes melting, sweet and sugary, like the marshmallows we threaded onto crooked twigs and held over a flickering campfire.

How could I possibly resist those lips that searched for mine? As the night descended to the sound of squeaking bats flying overhead, their flapping wings skimming the treetops.

You pressed your back against the moss-covered wooden planks of a decaying boat shed. A shimmering moon swimming in the still waters of the rippling lake. Your hand reaching down, hitching up your skirt. My hand pulling your panties to one side.

We fucked.

Your legs wrapped around my waist, hips pushing hard into me, mouth slowly opening, a lock of black curly hair falling across your flushed cheeks.

—

We sat on the grassy bank, reeds swaying in rhythm to the chorus of early morning birdsong.

Your head resting on my shoulder, my finger tracing the contour of your neck.

If only time could stop and this happiness last forever.

—

"*When I'm with you, love needs no explanation. It just is and we just are.*"

Ocean

I have cried an ocean for you, but still your ship refuses to sail.

How Love Feels

A lull in the storm. The sparkle of sunshine held by the rain. This is how love feels. Just when you thought everything was lost.

WRITER'S BLOCK

There was something quite perverse about my love of crisp, cold days, especially the ones touched by a weak, watery warmth that spilled down from skies of winter blue.

Perhaps it was the feeling of detachment found in remoteness that appealed to me.

Sitting in an empty park surrounded by the towering trees, bare and lonely—their leaves long departed and now left decaying on the chilly ground.

Even the odd flap of wings from startled sparrows, darting between bare limbs and withered branches, did little to interrupt the stillness of this solitary moment.

Where I found myself struggling to write poetry with scrawly pencil strokes. The faint gray words scattered across the pristine pages of a battered leather-bound journal.

Every sentence formed—a furrow plowed across an empty field.

Where seeds refused to grow.

I remember many years ago finding myself transfixed and strangely hypnotized by the mechanical whirring of an antique automaton.

Two metal monkeys with grimaced faces, covered in speckled paint and tuffs of tatty black hair. Sitting opposite each other. Weary combatants dueling across a wooden chessboard.

I watched as their arthritic metal paws moved the pieces with robotic precision. Playing the same game over and over again with the identical conclusion. After every checkmate, they reset the pieces to start playing again, only stopping to be rewound by the turn of an ornate brass key.

A beautiful exercise in futility—repetitive but strangely cathartic. Like a pencil driven between the blue lines of a journal by a driver with no clear direction in mind.

A throaty bark from a panting dog broke the silence.

Its muddy paws kicking up leaves. Bushy tail wagging as it chased a green tennis ball thrown by a loved-up couple, wearing his and hers matching blue hoodies.

I watched them walk away.

A trail of faint laughter clinging to a tangled thread of wispy breeze. A distant memory forming in my head with every step they took.

A last kiss stolen from Lucy's tear-stained lips.

Salty and unforgiving.

Her hand slowly slipping away from mine as we sat on this park bench.

The finality of her parting words.

"I love you, but, I just can't live with you anymore."

A miserable ending to our magnificent love story.

One that my pencil still refuses to write.

Romance

Romance seldom happens overnight. Sometimes, we have to grow the roses before we can give them.

Tokoriki

Here it is—
    my island,
    the sweet scent
    of frangipani,
    carried in the arms
    of a gentle breeze,
    serenaded by a sea—
    beating a slow rhythm
    on a golden drum.

How beautiful the moon—
    rising in balmy skies,
    where stars tumble
    into luminescent waves
    breaking on a distant reef.

Your body bathing
    in its light,
    skin the color
    of silver,
    reading Murakami
    by candlelight.

Memories—
    like a siren's song,
    calling me back
    to this place,
    where lovers
    come home.

Risk Everything

How precarious the fine line between acceptance and rejection. Yet here I am again—placing another bet on the table. Going all in. Willing to risk everything for a chance to win this stupid game we call love.

Smoke & Mirrors

She loved to eat strawberry jam on toast.

This gorgeous girl in a white dressing gown, gliding across the black-and-white-checkered kitchen floor like a ballerina on roller skates. Her blond hair tied in a ponytail and just a hint of pale pink lipstick glistening on those sweet lips.

Vivaldi's *The Four Seasons* rising up from the speakers of a 1980s Bang & Olufsen stereo that could still spin the dusty vinyl with perfect precision.

I could feel the gentle warmth of the morning sunshine on my unshaven cheek as it streamed in through the windows, sending dancing shadows across my coffee cup. My well-worn copy of *Alice's Adventures in Wonderland* open on the white marble benchtop.

Justine sat down next to me, picked up my cup, and took a sip.

"Don't you ever get bored of reading that book?" she asked, head peering over my shoulder.

"No, never. I love the absurdity and nonsense. I think of it as a pleasant escape from the dreary headlines in the morning papers.

Did you check on the fire? Has it died out yet?"

We had spent the previous night in the little courtyard garden, wrapped in blankets, poking the glowing embers of a fire with sticks, readying the flames for the next article of clothing to be plucked from a green garbage bag. The final remains of James laid to rest.

"It's still smoldering. Well, it was when I last looked earlier. I'll rake the ashes after breakfast and hose it down just to make doubly sure," she said.

"Don't worry about it. I'll take care of it," I replied, taking her hand and gently kissing the back of it.

—

I'd always known Justine as Justine. Even back in the days as university students, when we used to skip our lectures and go surf a curling left-hand break at Rocky Bay. Both of us sporting identical crew cuts, munching down on hot dogs, sitting on the sand, and laughing about our career prospects.

Somehow, we managed to scrape enough grades together to graduate. Justine moved away to New York to take a job as an intern in a law firm. I stayed behind to start a design company, my arts degree framed and hung on the wall of my bedroom.

As the years passed, I had gotten married and divorced, sold my design business, and eventually landed a job as an art director for a top New York advertising agency.

At some point during that time, Justine and I also lost touch with each other.

Until one spring afternoon, while I was eating a hot dog in Central Park, a familiar voice jolted me out of my daydream.

"What are you doing here, you loser?"

I spun around and almost fell off the park bench with surprise. Standing behind me was this gorgeous woman, dressed in a chic, navy blue pinstriped jacket and matching skirt. Her long blond hair caught by the wind and a black briefcase held in her hand. I knew who it was in an instant and felt a wave of joy sweep over my body.

We hugged and talked nonstop until the sun went down. Catching up on each other's news.

Justine was now a partner at a Midtown law firm and had inherited a brownstone on the Upper West Side from a wealthy aunt. I mentioned I was staying in a hotel while hunting for a new rental apartment. She was having none of that and insisted I stay at her place.

One week turned into a month and the rest, as they say, is history.

—

"Hello, is anyone at home?" Justine waved her hand in front of my face, snapping me out of my daydream.

I reached for my coffee cup and realized it was empty.

"My bad," Justine giggled. "But you were just staring into space, and I couldn't help myself. I'll put another pot on."

"Okay, thanks. I'll go check on the fire while you do that."

One of the nicest things about a Sunday morning was that feeling of inner peace. Knowing you didn't have to rush or do anything in particular.

I unbolted the twin glass doors that led into the courtyard, which was a patch of grass with a border of white rose bushes and a green wrought-iron outdoor table with two chairs sitting in the middle.

The blackened, charred remains of the fire had made a mess of the lawn. Wisps of gray smoke tainting the fresh scent of autumn air. I uncoiled the hose, turned on the squeaky brass tap, and dampened the area with a burst of water. My mind racing back to Saturday morning.

—

We had found the old, battered suitcase while cleaning out the attic. One of the many "must-do" tasks we had put off doing for over a year. It had been filled with junk stored by Justine's deceased aunt, covered in cobwebs, and home to a dead rat that we found lying next to a pile of old *Vogue* magazines.

How the suitcase had ended up in the attic was a mystery to Justine. She thought she had thrown it out long ago, but her aunt must have hung on to it.

When I opened it, a shocked expression washed over Justine's face, like she had come face-to-face with a ghost. Inside were clothes—his clothes, the ones she used to wear when she first arrived in New York and work colleagues knew her as James.

I could see the sadness in Justine's eyes as she picked through the folded trousers, business shirts, ties, socks, and underwear. It was like we had dug up a time capsule filled with all the memories she had wanted to forget.

Transporting her back to that brief period when living a lie seemed preferable to being true to herself. Before she found the courage to finally become the woman she always was.

I put my arms around Justine and held her tight while she sobbed into my shoulder.

I still felt a pang of guilt for not being there for her while she was going through the transformation, the gender realignment therapy and surgery. But like she told me, it was a journey she wanted to do alone, and that's why she had decided to cut off all ties to her previous life. Including me.

We emptied the contents of the suitcase into a large garbage bag and decided to light a fire. We spent the night burning all the clothes while swigging whiskey from a bottle and sharing stories about our old university days.

I remembered the very first time she told me her big secret. It was at a summer beach party, and we had been introduced to each other by a friend of mine. Right from the start, we just clicked.

We ended up smoking a joint in the dunes, watching the waves break. Chatting about surfing, gaming, and other stuff. And then midconversation, the words suddenly spilled out.

"Have you any idea what it feels like to be a woman trapped in the body of a man?"

At first, I wasn't sure how to react. I think I made some kind of stupid joke about how it was just my luck to meet a girl at a party who dressed like a dude. We both laughed, and from that point onward I always accepted James as Justine and our friendship grew.

But the truth was, I had no idea how it felt to be her; how could I?

—

Justine came out to the courtyard holding a cup of freshly brewed coffee.

A lock of blond hair falling down her forehead, the strands glowing in the sunlight.

"Here you go," she said, handing me the white china cup. Her eyes suddenly spotting the tears rolling down my cheeks. "Hey, what's wrong?"

She took the cup back from my hands and placed it down on the table.

"I'm so sorry."

I felt her arms wrap around my waist as she pulled me tightly into a warm embrace.

"I'm so sorry, Justine," I repeated. "I never should have let you go. I should have been there for you, stayed with you, protected you."

"Stop. Look at me," she said, cupping my face in the palms of her hands. Her eyes welling up with tears. "You were always there for me, and the only thing that matters is that you're here with me now. It was my decision to leave, but it was fate that brought us back together. God, I never thought I would ever get to know what happiness feels like. Never believed for a second I would find true love in this cold and callous world. But I did. We did. I love you. I love you more than life itself."

—

Her lips pressed against mine, and we kissed like never before. A new fire lit, but this time, deep within our hearts.

Both of us tumbling down a rabbit hole where Wonderland waited.

Far away from a past that no longer haunted us.

To this beautiful place.

Where smoke and mirrors ceased to exist.

(Can Survive Wednesday?)

Sara

(Last Verse)
Holding hands beneath
tangerine skies,
a sea of rolling fire
and flying fish,
a daydream made real
in the shutter click
of an eyelid

I believe in you   What if Sophie is killed
in a car crash?
Words that
water flowers
Peace

elegance

Dinner
at Café Hawa

Burn all the Dictionaries
tear up the fixed metaphors
tell the Poets to go to hell —

Only the Heart

One of the most gorgeous delusions is actually believing love can be explained with words. Only the heart can understand its true meaning.

UNKNOWN PLEASURES

Pearly suns—
  buttons undone,
  one by one,
  in a garden
  of wild orchids.

On bended knees—
  your fingertips,
  with open lips,
  give ecstasy
  a name.

STICKY TAPE

My fingers pull
    clear sticky tape
    from nipples,
    just as you orgasm—
    how exquisite
    the pleasure found,
    in so little pain.

Waiting for Love

Love can often be like waiting for a train to arrive and then suddenly realizing you're standing on the wrong platform.

THE WEDDING ALBUM

You are magic in moonlight.

A sun-kissed siren
    laughing on a pebbled beach.

The lost love in a love song
    playing on my headphones.

A sheep in wolf's clothing
    running away from herself.

My hand turning back time
    with every page turned—
    to the last photograph.

Two broken performers
    in a three-person pantomime.

Our happiness scattered—
    the torn wings of butterflies
    fluttering in the wind.

Like cursed confetti
    thrown by the hand
    of a bitter bridesmaid.

On the unhappiest
    of happy days.

Empty Words

There are plenty
    of other fish in the sea,
    you said sitting by
    the ocean,
    never knowing
    what it's like
    to live your life
    in a shrinking pond—
    fast becoming
    an empty puddle.

Femme Fatale

She unclipped the pretty black bra and flashed me a wry smile. Her eyes possessed that rarest of qualities, a sparkle of mischief with just a hint of danger. And when she spoke, her words circled me, like hungry wolves moving in for the kill.

—

"I can't stop thinking about last night," she whispered. "I felt like a pinball machine. Your fingers hitting all the right buttons, bells ringing, my body lit up and begging for a replay."

ONE KISS

All it took was one kiss.

The tide running backward away
from the beach.

Our love—

An unstoppable force building
on the horizon.

Two hearts stranded on the shore.

Waiting for the tsunami to hit.

I LOVE YOU

The most beautiful
    sound in the world to me
    is not forest birdsong
    or babbling brooks
    or even the ringing
    of church bells.

It's hearing you
    whisper "I love you"
    over and over again.

Behind the Laundromat

You laughed when my hands touched you. Wandering fingers tickling goose-bumped thighs. Opening the invitation I wrote. Feeling the wet reply between your legs.

THE UNPALATABLE TRUTH

It came as no surprise,
    our recipe for love
    would end up ruined.

Half-baked truths
    burnt to a crisp—
    on the lowest setting.

Always coming back
    for second helpings.

Choosing to eat shit
    rather than go hungry.

WAKE UP

When did opinions become more important than facts?

How did science get replaced by ignorance and conspiracy theories? Why is the world so divided, torn apart, and broken?

What the fuck happened to humanity while we were asleep with our eyes wide open?

Where did common sense and unity go to die?

—

Social media.

LET IT GO

Never let anger get the better of you. No matter how justified it might seem at the time, in hindsight, it seldom solves or changes anything for the better. Find the courage to forgive yourself, even if you can't forgive them.

The Saddest Truth

The saddest truth is realizing you have fallen madly in love with what can never be.

Cult of One

I've always been fascinated with cults.

Not necessarily the kind that hit the newspaper headlines, where maniacal bearded leaders deliver death to their grinning devotees. But more the everyday, almost invisible cults. The ones we find ourselves hopelessly drawn toward and frequently get trapped in.

Like the drunk buying a bottle of booze on a Monday morning.

The religious zealot who confuses faith with certainty and attacks others for not sharing the same belief as them. Political junkies who divide the world into left and right. Hurling insults at each other from the trenches while the politicians line their pockets with thirty pieces of silver.

How we pin posters of pop idols and movie stars to our bedroom walls. Stalk the followed on social media. Wait patiently in the pouring rain, just to catch a glimpse of passing stardom. Screaming fans intoxicated by fame, addicted to celebrity— *monkeys watching other monkeys eat bananas.*

And then there's our endless pursuit for the next shiny trinket.

Fallen angels shopping for halos. Worshipping at the crumbling altar of commercialism. Emptying wallets and bankrupting our souls.

But perhaps it's the Cult of Two that interests me the most.

Where we chase butterflies disguised as romantic dreams—*the relentless desire to love and be loved in return.*

Running from one relationship to the next. Hoping this time it will be different. Always forgetting that love is unpredictable, complicated, and wonderful in equal parts.

And when we come up empty-handed, we can't wait to push the self-destruct button.

Like how when a relationship ends, we often needlessly blame ourselves. Or waste even more of our precious energy pointing the finger at the other person. Rather than simply letting go and moving on—the ultimate act of retribution.

The truth is, the harsh reality of love is that it's fickle, mostly fleeting, and seldom ticks every single box if we do find it.

Just as we have to come to terms with our own inherent flaws, we need to be open to accepting the limitations of others. This doesn't mean we have to sell ourselves short or subscribe to second best. It's more about recognizing our individual differences and asking ourselves, *Can we honestly make this relationship work?*

Real love is not just the willingness to make it happen but also the absolute certainty that it can.

So please don't rush into love or put your life on hold waiting for it. Enjoy being blissfully single. Use this precious time to really get to know yourself. To discover who you are, what you really want—*and the future you so fucking deserve.*

While you're on this gorgeous inward adventure, go explore the wonderful world outside your bedroom window. Run away with the circus and never look back. Leave behind all the dumb expectations society expects of you, the bullshit others put on you, and create your own destiny.

Just be you.

In your amazing, dazzling, beautifully crazy—Cult of One.

—

Do you believe it's possible to find true love?

Yes—because I found you.

Unravel

I want to feel your fingers unclip my bra, she said, and unravel the last thread of decency I possess.

One More Touch

I love how your hips rise, reaching the point of no return, fingers gripping the sheets—my hand between your legs.

Second Helping

It was past 3 a.m. when Todd stumbled through the front door of the apartment and staggered into the bedroom. The familiar naughty boy grin plastered across his face as he rocked back and forth at the end of the bed. The stench of cheap liquor and stale cigarettes on his breath.

Sarah was sitting up in the bed, dressed in her favorite pink flannel dressing gown. She put down the cookbook she was reading and stared at Todd's bloodshot eyes.

"I'm sorry, babe. Got caught up with the boys again and lost track of time," he slurred.

"That's okay. How about you get undressed and into bed. You must be exhausted," Sarah said softly.

Todd flashed a crooked smirk as he collapsed onto the bed next to her like a sack of old rags. His head hitting the pillow. Eyes closing shut as he passed out.

Sarah hopped out of bed and took off his muddy shoes. She gently folded her half of the white comforter over him and left the bedroom, switching off the light on her way out.

It wasn't the first time Sarah had been forced to sleep on the sofa. She pulled a blanket over her body, rested her head on a cushion, and stared up at the ceiling, listening in the dark to Todd's thunderous snoring coming from the bedroom.

—

It was late in the morning, and the sun was streaming through the kitchen window.

Sarah checked her watch and wandered over to the oven. Peering through the glass door, she could see the golden crust of the pie and knew it was ready. She reached for the oven gloves from the counter and put them on.

When the pie came out of the oven, Sarah eyed it with a satisfied smile. It was perfectly cooked and filled the entire ceramic baking dish. She placed it down on the stove top and reached up for a white dinner plate from the shelf.

"Ooh, my fucking head!"

Sarah heard Todd's chesty moan coming from the bedroom, followed by a loud, rumbling fart. He was finally awake.

She neatly cut a generous slice of the pie and placed it on the plate with a spatula. She carried it quickly into the bedroom with a small bottle of water she had taken from the fridge.

Todd was still in his disheveled suit, greasy hair flopped over his forehead, trying to summon up the strength to crawl out of bed.

"I thought you might want breakfast in bed, sweetheart," Sarah said, placing the plate down in front of him.

Todd reached over and snatched the bottle of water from her hand.

He unscrewed the cap and poured the water into his throat, gulping it down and throwing the empty bottle onto the carpet. He looked at the slice of pie sitting on the plate.

"Smells bloody marvelous," he exclaimed, grinning.

"Let me go get you a knife and fork," Sarah replied.

"Nah, fuck that. I'll use my hands."

Sarah watched Todd tear the pie apart with his chubby fingers, shoving large mouthfuls of pastry into his mouth—the thick brown gravy running down the stubble on his chin.

"What is it? Beef? Tastes a bit like chicken too."

"Oh, it's just a little something I whipped up. A new recipe," Sarah said. "I hope you like it."

Todd burped and wiped his sticky fingers on the comforter. "Like it? I fucking love it! Be a good girl and go get me another slice."

Sarah dutifully picked up the dirty plate off the bed and returned to the kitchen, where she cut another large slice of the pie before walking back into the bedroom.

"There you go, sweetheart. Enjoy!"

She handed Todd the plate and watched him start to devour the second helping of pie. He smacked his lips as he swallowed large chunks of gristle and soggy meat.

Sarah left him to finish eating his breakfast.

When she got back to the kitchen, she looked down at her gold wedding ring. She let out a little sigh and slid it off her finger. Throwing it into the trash can.

The ring rattled against the sides of the empty cans of cheap dog food sitting inside.

Sarah couldn't hold back the smile any longer and chuckled to herself.

A wave of euphoria swept through her body as she skipped across the living room to the front door where her packed suitcase lay waiting.

She picked it up and quietly slipped out of the apartment.

A Slow Pirouette

You took my hand and made it yours. Guiding my fingers beneath the hem of your panties. Showing me exactly how you wanted to be touched—like a ballerina in the spotlight doing a slow pirouette.

Vanishing Act

Where did our love go? The rabbit no longer visible under the top hat. Just an empty space to remind me how quickly our eyes can be deceived, and a broken heart left unanswered.

In Vain

I tried so many times to reach out to you—before I realized that seemingly tiny space between our outstretched fingertips was in reality a chasm.

MOUSETRAPS

My head—
    a dusty attic,
    filled with faded
    love letters,
    and forgotten
    mousetraps.

Yet here I am,
    thinking of you again—
    eyes closed,
    walking barefoot,
    reliving the pain
    with every step.

SCREAMING SEX

Swirling smoke
   from the last drag
   on a dying joint.

You strike a pose
   wearing black leather
   crotchless panties.

Giving me—*that look*.

Doe-eyed innocence
   meets bitten lip.

Beautifully perverse,
   breathtaking—
   a silent surrender.

Screaming sex
   without saying
   a single word.

Black Stockings

You were naked.

Except for a pair of sheer black stockings you wore with matching heels. Sitting on a hard wooden chair with your knees apart.

"I have a little surprise for you."

I watched as your fingers reached down and slowly tore a hole in the crotch of the stockings. Your eyes never leaving mine as more of your pussy was exposed with each rip of the fabric.

"Shame to ruin such a pretty pair of stockings," I replied.

Sophia laughed and opened her legs wider.

"Well, perhaps it's your turn to ruin me."

—

"Do you think I'm kinky?"

"No. I think you're a girl blessed with a vivid imagination."

Winter of Summers

I don't think either of us was searching for anyone. We were just two lost souls drawn together by circumstance. Travelers walking along the same stretch of lonely road, the well-trodden path to redemption. Looking for meaning in this meaningless life. Strangers who became more than just friends over a bottle of vodka in a bar, sheltering from a blizzard.

The next morning, we moved what little possessions we carried in our backpacks into a cabin by the frozen lake. Handing over a month's rent to the grizzled man wearing a rabbit fur hat. His eyebrow raised when we said we weren't married. Lighting a crumpled cigarette between his wrinkled lips as he pointed out the dusty furniture, dented fridge, little gas cooker, and fireplace. Walking us into the tiny bedroom and patting the bed with his giant hand, a small sneer creeping across his rugged face.

Rachel smiled awkwardly. I felt my cheeks blushing red. We hadn't crossed this line yet, where kisses became so much more.

"I'll leave you two to settle in. Don't forget to prime the water pump and keep the generator topped up in case the power goes," he said in a deep voice.

We nodded like anxious children in front of a scary headmaster, trying our best to hide the fact we honestly didn't have a clue what he was talking about. A wave of relief sweeping over us as the old man pulled the creaky front door closed behind him.

"Left or right side?" Rachel asked laughing. Her nervousness disguised with playful banter as she hopped onto the bed, making the decision for me.

—

The weeks passed slowly as we both slipped easily into the roles of make-believe lovers.

I spent most days camped on the tatty brown sofa, head buried in a book, cooking in the evenings and only venturing away from the cabin to visit the general store in town. To withdraw cash from the ATM, pick up groceries, and buy bottles of wine. My savings account was well topped up by the sale of my apartment back in Vancouver. A place where my old life lay in ruins. Another time, a different story.

Rachel was far more industrious. Waking at dawn to write on her laptop, a collection of poetry she hoped to turn into a book one day. Her way of making sense of a broken marriage, she told me. A cathartic journey taken with fingers that had spent too much time wiping away tears from her soft gray eyes. When she wasn't writing, and the sun was shining, she would be outside building snowmen. Using carrots to give them erect cocks. Laughing at my frequent eye rolls whenever I discovered a new one.

The nights we spent playing cards with an old deck we had found in a wooden chest of drawers, along with a large collection of '70s porn magazines. Not that we needed any encouragement to fuck.

It became one of our regular evening activities. So much so, it caused our old bed to break, a leg suddenly snapping, sending us rolling off the mattress onto the floor. After the initial shock of landing on our bare asses, all we could do was giggle. Rachel, always the resourceful one, managed to prop up the bed with a log found in the firewood pile. After that mini-disaster, we kept the bed solely for sleeping. Choosing instead to have sex everywhere else in the cabin. We even did it outside one afternoon. Up against a tree that towered above the roof and threatened to come crashing down every time a fierce storm hit.

Yet for all the physical intimacy, we were still mysteries to each other.

I had tried not to bore Rachel with the nitty-gritty of my doomed relationship, and she was always reluctant to talk about her past. When I did once ask her about her husband, she quickly shut me down with a frosty glare and screamed, "You don't need to know, just leave it at that!" So I kept things simple, lighthearted, and wonderfully superficial.

—

One Friday morning I did the unforgivable.

While Rachel was outside ice fishing on the lake, I took a quick peek through the pile of pages she had written. Nervously peering out of the frosty window every so often, just in case I would be caught in the act. I knew what I was doing was wrong, but curiosity got the better of my decency.

There was one particular piece that jumped out at me.

Revenge

Did you feel the blade?
cold metal slicing
through butter skin,
your blood—
the color of strawberry jam,
sticky upon my fingers.

The gurgling opera of death—
such sweet notes
played on a red stage,
soft murmurings
of a cheating heart,
slowly stilled to silence,
a throat cut,
eyes rolling backward.

To think I loved you once—
my dearest dead husband,
never to rest in peace,
and when you burn
in the fires of Hell,
think of me—
the girl whose life
you took first.

While I read the lines for a second time, little did I know just how quickly *a dark serendipity* would change everything in an instant.

The distant wailing of police sirens made my body jolt upright, the page falling out of my hands. My head spun back to the window. I could see the silhouette of Rachel getting out of her chair and standing up on the blanket of icy white.

I felt the hairs rise on the back of my neck. My heart sinking as I raced out the front door and ran toward the lake. A couple of police cars skidded to a halt near me. I heard the noise of an ice drill starting up.

As I got closer to Rachel, I could see what she was doing. Her arms vibrating as she frantically cut away at the hole in the ice, making it wider.

"Rachel!" I screamed, a large cloud of breath exploding from my lips.

Rachel dropped the drill and stared in my direction. A quiet smile breaking across her rosy cheeks. Behind me I could hear voices yelling. I turned around and saw the police coming, guns drawn, and a barking dog tugging at its leash, held by the old man who had rented us the place.

I looked back at Rachel, panic surging through me, only to be met again by that serene smile.

Michael Faudet

"I'll never forget you." Her words reaching me before I could wrap my arms around her.

In a matter of seconds, she was gone. Not even a splash of water to mark her descent into the hole, as she plunged feetfirst under the lake.

To be lost forever.

—

How can I forget the warmth of your body, the love that burned brightly within our hearts? You were my winter of summers.

Paris

I'm not a complicated girl, she laughed. I just want to run away with you, rob a bank, fall in love, and eat ice cream in Paris.

You and Me

You once told me that the shortest distance between two points is a straight line. Unfortunately, the same can't be said for finding love.

I Had No Idea

A light rain shower
  in bright sunshine—
  that's how you
  hid your sadness,
  my eyes blinded
  by your smile,
  mistaking the tears
  for happiness.

Venus

I can still remember the hot summer night we sat by the lake, beads of water clinging to our naked skin, while a full moon rose from the shadows of swaying forest trees. My head resting on your shoulder as you pointed out Venus, our words whispered, a love story written by stars.

—

"When you look into my eyes, what do they say?"

"I'm obsessed with you. Utterly, willingly, and wonderfully so."

In Love with Words

I'm not just in love with words, I'm possessed by them. My life consumed by the twenty-six letters of the alphabet and all the countless possibilities they bring to a page. How beautiful this world of dust and cobwebs. Where the pen is mightier than the vacuum cleaner.

FREEDOM

Run towards your dream, and never let anyone fill your pockets with rocks.

Her Little Secret

I know it's wrong,
    but the very thought
    of your hands,
    reaching up under
    my skirt
    and touching me,
    makes me blush
    in all the right places.

DEVOTION

Every Sunday—
    a sermon served,
    in silk robes
    and silver rings.

The gold plate
    passed around—
    collecting coins
    from empty pockets.

Come Monday—
    we work for
    our daily bread.

Bought with sweat
    and broken backs.

Praying—
    for a miracle.

PRETTY TORMENTS

I love,
   how you like
   to tease.

Slowly crawling,
   while your legs
   do the talking,
   with knees
   that blush,
   on wooden floors.

Dropping a pencil,
   and picking it up.

AFTER THE PARTY

A sweet hint
   of summer strawberries,
   on glistening lips
   stained sticky red.

Our first kiss—
   under a waning moon,
   adrift in a sea
   of silent black.

A bra strap falls,
   breathy notes
   by fingers played—
   on blades of green
   beneath twisted trees.

A whisper of silk
   on midnight thigh,
   as panties drop
   with gentle sigh.

DYING ROSES

Time to shine—
    in the brilliance
    of unbridled youth.

To see the future
    with wonderous eyes,
    looking forward
    and never back.

To kiss with lips
    that sip happiness
    from a silver chalice.

Filled to the brim
    with the nectar
    of sweet naivety.

To always question
    the reason why,
    but not the when.

To live a life
    of beautiful delusion.

Like dying roses
    worshipping the sun.

THE END OF THE BEGINNING

Some days it seemed that life couldn't get any better.

Like that photo of you on my screensaver. Standing by the billowing entrance to the white canvas big top. Clowning around and pulling faces to the camera. Holding a stick of pink cotton candy in the falling rain.

But then there were other days, when it felt like the circus had run away from us.

Leaving us alone to unpack the future and seek meaning in the emptiness. Finding ourselves abandoned on this stupid rotating planet. Lost in a world of endless spin.

Constantly self-medicating with daily doses of alternative reality.

Desperately trying to decipher twinkling code sent from dying stars. Reading oolong tea leaves in empty teacups. Frantically searching for hidden messages in the license plates of passing cars.

Anything to escape the nonsense of the nightly news—the insanity of a civil war fought with fingertips on social media.

Often coming to the uncomfortable conclusion that none of us was really woke. Just sleepwalking automata wound up to the breaking point.

Pushing and shoving our way to the front of the line.

Banging on the gates of a fucked-up carnival and begging to be let in. Paying the ultimate price of admission by stealing the last few coins of freedom from each other's pockets.

But some nights it seemed like none of this really mattered. Those precious evenings when love really did conquer all—and every kiss felt like therapy.

Taking us back to that innocent place we once knew. Where glorious summer days went to die.

Living in a paradise of blissful naivety with the scent of youth on our skin.

Your hands playing with matches.

THANK YOU

I cannot express how cathartic it feels to have my life, once held so tightly by the pages of five books, be finally set free in just one.

And I'm truly grateful to have you by my side to share this thrilling experience.

Reading the very words I wrote through the change of seasons— the passing of years.

As you would expect, I reluctantly had to leave some poetry and prose behind. Possibly one of your favorites, and certainly plenty of mine.

But such is the dilemma when brevity keeps time.

So, if you find yourself craving a little more, you can read the rest of my writing in my other books: *Dirty Pretty Things*, *Bitter Sweet Love*, *Smoke & Mirrors*, *Winter of Summers*, and *Cult of Two*.

Please feel free to tell your friends about *Playing with Matches*.

And naturally, I'd also love to hear from you too.

We can stay in touch on my official Facebook, Twitter, and Instagram pages.

Thanks again for all your wonderful support.

Best wishes always,

—Michael xo

ACKNOWLEDGMENTS

A big thank you to my agent, Alec Shane, who not only made this book happen but also provided me with all the support a writer could possibly need during a global pandemic. I truly appreciate all the hard work done too by the rest of the team at Writers House, New York.

To Al Zuckerman, who took me on this publishing journey, and made the best Negronis ever, I thank you for all the fun times we spent together.

A warm thank you to Kirsty Melville, Patty Rice, and Kathy Hilliard for doing what you do so well. I look forward to the time when COVID is vanquished, and we can all meet up again to celebrate this sixth book with Andrews McMeel. Shots of Tito's vodka I think would be most appropriate.

Malika Favre, thank you for your genius, generosity, and wicked sense of humor. I adore the visual magic you conjured up to create the cover of *Playing with Matches*. Magnifique!

To my son, Oliver, how crazy to think that by the time this book hits the bookstores, you will be heading off to university. I'm so proud of you and love you more than all the dumplings you've ever eaten, and likely to eat in the future. (I'll leave you to calculate that number.)

Mum, Dad, Genevieve, and Ryder, I have missed you terribly while preparing this book. When New Zealand closed its borders to the world, I had no idea it would be for so long. But thankfully there is now light at the end of this tunnel. I can't wait to see your smiling faces again and to finally meet Nora, the new addition to your dog family.

To my friends, you know who you are, time to socialize again! Reservations being taken now for dinner at Ghost Street if you're up for it.

My last thank-you is for the person who deserves it the most.

The love of my life.

Lang.

About the Author

Michael Faudet is the author of the international bestsellers *Dirty Pretty Things*, *Bitter Sweet Love*, *Smoke & Mirrors*, *Winter of Summers*, and *Cult of Two*. His books have been nominated in the Goodreads Choice Awards for Best Poetry. *Dirty Pretty Things* was also selected by Sylvia Whitman, the owner of the iconic Shakespeare and Company bookstore in Paris, as one of her personal favorite books of 2016.

Michael frequently explores the intricacies of love, loss, relationships, and sex in poetry, prose, and short stories. His lyrical and often sensual writing continues to attract readers from all around the world.

Before turning his hand to writing books, Michael enjoyed a successful career in advertising as an award-winning executive creative director. He managed creative departments and developed advertising campaigns for major brands in many countries.

Michael is represented by the literary agency Writers House, New York. He currently lives in New Zealand in a little house by the sea with girlfriend and author Lang Leav.

Michael Faudet

INDEX

Michael Faudet

Follow Michael Faudet on social media:

Andrews McMeel Publishing
a division of Andrews McMeel Universal
1130 Walnut Street, Kansas City, Missouri 64106

www.andrewsmcmeel.com

www.michaelfaudet.com

21 22 23 24 25 VEP 10 9 8 7 6 5 4 3 2 1

ISBN: 978-1-5248-6989-2

Library of Congress Control Number: 2021944363

Cover design and illustration by Malika Favre

Editor: Patty Rice
Art Director/Designer: Julie Barnes
Production Editor: Dave Shaw
Production Manager: Cliff Koehler

ATTENTION: SCHOOLS AND BUSINESSES
Andrews McMeel books are available at quantity discounts with bulk purchase for educational, business, or sales promotional use. For information, please e-mail the Andrews McMeel Publishing Special Sales Department: specialsales@amuniversal.com.